The MUSIC of ETERNITY

Everyday Sounds of Fidelity

ADRIAN VAN KAAM

AVE MARIA PRESS
Notre Dame, Indiana 46556

C. 2

© 1990 by The Epiphany Association

International Standard Book Number: 0-87793-436-3
                                      0-87793-435-5 (pbk.)

Library of Congress Catalog Card Number: 90-82096

Cover and text design by Elizabeth J. French

Printed and bound in the United States of America.

Acknowledgments

A book is never the work of one person alone.

I want to offer my sincere thanks to Dr. Susan Muto, currently executive director of the Epiphany Association and an adjunct professor at Duquesne University's Institute of Formative Spirituality, for responding to my request to review the manuscript carefully and to suggest improvements in language and content. I express my gratitude as well to her aunt, Eve Bauer, who expertly and patiently typed several revisions of the text. Their commitment over several months to the task of bringing this book to completion speaks to its main theme, in a word, how faithfulness to daily happenings, viewed from a transcendent perspective, leads to a vibrant life replete with peace and joy.

I also want to thank members of the Epiphany Association who week after week followed ongoing spiritual formative sessions based on selected chapters, testing the validity of their contents in dialogue with their daily lives. Their response to the "music of eternity" in great measure led to significant additions to original writings and enhanced especially the closing prayer-poems. To each and all I acknowledge my gratefulness and personal blessings.

Contents

5

Introduction

It is 1944-1945, the last year of World War II, in the besieged Netherlands. The allied troops defeated in the Battle of Arnhem have given up the plan to liberate the west and north of my country. German troops dig in, stocks of food are taken away, thousands of men are transported to work camps, others are rounded up for execution or concentration camps. Famine sets in, numerous people die from hunger. Many escape to the countryside. I find myself among them in a small village called Nieuwkoop. I am 24 years old, a theology student in the last year before ordination. Desperate people hiding with me come to me for counsel. After all, I am a "man of the cloth," at least in final preparation, so I must know how to help them. Their plight forces me into a practical speed course in spiritual counseling. Their trust fires my thinking. It sets me on a new course for life.

Their plight is that many of them have lost their homes, their jobs, their confidence in life. Others, especially Jewish friends I helped to hide, have lost wives, husbands, children, parents and friends in gas chambers and dungeons. The form they gave to their life in better times is falling apart. My first task is to help them get themselves together. The future seems hopeless. The only hope I can enkindle in them is faith in a higher power. Different people of different faith

traditions experience that power in different ways.
However one names it, this connection with the
"More Than" helps them to go beyond their seem-
ingly insignificant, pain-filled point in time. We close
our ears to the rumors of disaster and try to hear inwardly the barely audible "music of eternity."

I tell them how this music comes through the
openings of everyday life. Even in this diaspora of desperate people, a diaspora threatened by the enemy's
destruction of the dikes that keep our lowlands from
drowning in the sea, the sound is heard. I call this
shining forth of eternity in daily people, in often unnoticed events and things, *epiphanies* of the higher power
that keep our hope alive.

I remind them of Japanese girls, who spend hours
shaping and arranging bouquets of flowers or practicing silent tea ceremonials. By being totally *with* what
they are doing, they not only give form to flowers and
drinking tea but also to their dispersed lives. In presence to a simple task at hand, they experience what
they are doing as an epiphany of a higher scheme of
things, as a theme in the music of eternity. They gather
together not only flowers but, in loving appreciation,
they also recollect their own thoughts, feelings, images, memories and anticipations. They become
whole again, able to form their limited life and that of
deprived others to a higher degree of peace and refinement.

I realize that we become split, tense and broken
when we give up the attempt to be simply and wholly
with and *in* the situation in which we find ourselves for
better or worse. The secret of not falling apart, of not
losing a meaningful way of life, is to try to be present to
the simple things and deeds that flow one to the other
during endless days of hiding together. To live these
moments as epiphanies of a higher power, as themes

of a concealed symphony always playing in the universe, is a pursuit worth every effort.

We begin to try to be "epiphanic" people, who give full attention to the things of everyday life as manifestations of a higher meaning, as gifts of an ever-present eternal love. We try to pay relaxed attention to the sounds of life—wind in the rafters of the attics of the farms in which so many are concealed; rain on the haystacks to which we flee when army units pass by; footsteps of farm hands in the stable feeding the cows; voices of children in the kitchen; whirring, churning machines making buttermilk. We learn to be attentive to appearances like a blade of grass, a humming insect, a small sparrow, the shape of a buttercup, the weather-beaten faces of old workers, the flowing lines of furniture or dress. To be epiphanic in this way helps us to gather ourselves together as living *here* and *now*. It means to live fully where we are, not to rush ahead to what may happen tomorrow or to sink back in a past that is no longer there.

For those of us who work in the resistance, epiphanic presence to the battle for justice makes us more effective. Ineffectiveness is often due to not being wholly with the things we are doing. When a resistance fighter sees his or her task as a noble sharing in the eternal cry for justice, involvement and attention grow by leaps and bounds. We do a better job.

Such relaxed epiphanic attention in daily life can deepen almost imperceptibly. With the aid of grace, it readies us for a more profound religious presence in tune with our faith. The epiphanic attitude becomes a principal graced condition for living a spiritual life.

After the war and my ordination, I discovered that many people in our postwar world had really fallen apart; they lost a good, well-balanced form of life. To grow beyond their dispersion, their low-grade depression, their lack of meaning, they, too, like those in hiding, needed the epiphanic disposition.

In the Netherlands and later in America, I tried to further develop and foster the epiphanic way of life as a condition for a coherent, deeply meaningful life formation. This attempt reached its finest possibility when I co-founded the Epiphany Association in 1979 with the help of Dr. Susan Muto. Dr. George Armstrong Kelly III, a professor and outstanding scholar in the philosophy of religion at Johns Hopkins University, a devout Episcopalian, was so inspired by the epiphany approach that he deeded to us the lovely Victorian house of his deceased aunt, Eleanor Park Kelly, a dedicated Presbyterian. The "Kelly House" was given to us under four conditions: 1) that we use it as a research, resource and publication center fostering the epiphany approach; 2) that it be in principle ecumenical, not restricted to only one denomination; 3) that the house, especially its ground floor and furniture, be kept in the aesthetic refinement his aunt asked our benefactor to protect in the future; 4) that the house and the epiphany activities centered in it maintain their independence from any bureaucratic organization, such as a company or university.

We assented gladly to these conditions. When Dr. Kelly saw how faithful we were to what we had promised, he helped us financially to better organize the consultation and communication outreach of our center. We have been researching, writing and publishing, giving conferences and workshops nationwide and internationally, to meet our goals. For example, the Association, under contract with the U.S. Navy, brought the epiphany message to 1,100 naval chaplains of 86 different faith groupings and recently accepted a contract with the U.S. Air Force to teach the same. A six-part series of videocassettes on *Becoming Spiritually Mature* is in the process of production. We can in gratitude say that God has blessed this work abundantly.

The music of eternity, the cosmos and its unfolding, humanity and its history, each unique person, you and I, all events that make up our life are in the loving heart of the Eternal. They all are in God as a wondrous symphony to be played out in eons of time and in our own passing lives.

The music of eternity—do you hear it coming through? Does it evoke in you joy and serenity? Does it enhance your readiness to be good to those who are deprived?

Or have you lost your ear for this music, your sensitivity to the divine meaning of all that happens to you, of every simple thing to which you are exposed? Are you perhaps more fascinated by the worldly meanings of people, events and things? The media, self-help books, education, commercials, novels, plays immerse us in what things mean for our pleasure, satisfaction, power, beauty, health and career. Their message is so loud that it deafens us to the subtle music of the divine. And yet the divine mystery appears everywhere, at every moment.

The Greeks coined the word "epiphany," appearance, to point to the manifestations of the gods. Christianity applied the word to *the* Word, to the Eternal Son becoming one of us in Bethlehem. Jesus is the Appearance of appearances of the Eternal—coming among us in a way no Greek or Roman could have dreamt about. All the music of eternity was expressed in the Eternal Son. It is meant to be expressed in the Christ, who would enter creation.

Do you hear the music of eternity in the Christ who permeates humanity and universe? Do you sense his epiphany everywhere? If you hear this music, do you try to live in fidelity to its tune?

Under the auspices of the Epiphany Association, I offer you this book of meditations on fidelity to the music of eternity, to the epiphanies in your life. I dedicate it to the memory of our beloved friend, the late Dr. George Kelly, whose faith, love and generosity were used by God to make our research, resource and communication center a vibrant reality. To him and to all the friends and supporters of this center, I dedicate this poem:

Epiphanies of Mystery

Bring gifts to life:
fields rife
with lustrous vegetation
swaying in winds of inspiration
to be epiphanies of Mystery.
Feel what it means
to rise as greens
no longer entombed and bound
as silent seeds
in sleeping ground.

—*Adrian van Kaam*
January, 1990

1

Fidelity to Daily Duty

Not long ago I talked with a mechanic employed in an airline maintenance crew. He told me of the fines airlines have to pay when their mechanics are found negligent in any way, for even a slight mistake endangers lives. The slightest indifference is already too much. "The sky will be safe," he said, "only when we love our job, when we care for travelers. Their lives rest in our hands. If you accept a job like this, you must feel responsible. You must be faithful to your duties, no matter your own mood and worries." He felt that such concern had diminished not only among maintenance crews, but in many occupations and, worst of all, in family life. "The quality of life is going down," he said. "People tend to be moody and mercurial; they do not live up to their responsibilities. You cannot count on them."

People may work for money, prestige and promotion—legitimate concerns to be sure—but these should be complemented by a sense of commitment. We should not look for an easy deal, for cutting corners. Otherwise, people cannot depend on us. Trust disappears. Without trust life becomes unlivable. Where there is no care, there is no trust. When profit prevails, compassion dies. If commitment is absent, neglect is present. When dedication wanes, life loses its sparkle.

The wisdom of this mechanic makes us aware of the need for fidelity in a world grown less reliable, less trustworthy. Fidelity to pacts and promises, to spouse and offspring, to friends, neighbors, church, school, place of work or political party is essential for human togetherness.

Fidelity goes deeper than doing things efficiently. A computer can beat us in that. Fidelity means much more. It means that our heart is in the doing. We are really "with it." We feel for what has to be done, for the people who depend on us and for the Lord who trusts in us. Fidelity makes us do things as well as we can without overconcern. Anxious concern conflicts with effectiveness. Fearfulness is not faithfulness. Relaxed fidelity is rooted in faith. Fidelity is called faithfulness. The fuller our faith, the greater our fidelity. Because faith has faltered, fidelity has weakened.

Jesus asks us to be faithful: "The Son of Man is coming at an hour you do not expect. Who, then, is the wise and trustworthy servant whom the master placed over his household to give them their food at the proper time? Blessed that servant if his master's arrival finds him doing exactly that. In truth I tell you, he will put him in charge of everything he owns" (Mt 24:44-46).

Thank you, Lord, for your appreciation of fidelity. At any time you may knock at the door of my heart. Make me ready to let you in, to sense the sound of your voice, the step of your feet. Make me welcome you. You may visit me at a time I least expect—the time of involvement in my daily task, in my family or community. The least expected time! I should not think that you only touch my heart when I am in church or saying my prayers. You may choose any moment of my day to be there for me in a special way. Who knows the time or the hour?

To serve you is to serve your friends in that little corner of your home which you entrusted to me. You make clear I can be faithful only if I am a far-sighted servant. It is difficult to be faithful if I keep my nose to the grindstone, if I see only the tediousness and disappointment that accompany all human endeavors. Grant me the gift of far-sightedness. Let me see beyond the appearance of my profession, family, neighborhood, school or parish. Nearsightedness can only discourage me. It paralyzes fidelity, the art of seeing beyond, of hearing a divine voice in everyday-ness.

Enable me to do what you ask me to in this gospel text: to dispense with loving care the kind of food I am called to give to those in need. It may be the food of airline maintenance for those in need of safety; of careful cleaning for those in need of sanitary washrooms; of wisdom for those in need of counsel; of justice for those in need of relief from oppression; of education for those in need of learning; of dance, music, painting, sculpture, poetry for those in need of beauty. As you predicted, all kinds of poverty will always be with us. Fidelity to my daily duty is my way of sharing with you the unfolding mystery of God's love for humanity.

The Faithful Heart

I
We daily bear
the wear and tear
of worried words,
their grinding power.
Pressures stored
in endless hours,
showers of obligations,
wages of the faithful life
of parent, husband, wife.

II

The busy patter
of little feet in our home,
they play, they laugh, they moan,
they are in need.
We have to feed
their mouths and minds.

III

May we be led
as you in Nazareth
by Father's will.
Celebrating silently
the dawn of mystery
in every little thing.

IV

You make them sing
a melody of praise
like all the little ways
we meet in daily care
and in the pain we bear
in surrender to your will.
A faithful heart is still
the center of the hurricane
of rise and wane
of daily chatter.

V

Be kind
let us unwind,
grant us abandonment
to the finite end
of everything
in space and time.
You only know
in love divine
the hidden mine
of healing treasures.

2

Human and Divine Fidelity

That is why he said, on coming into the world: "You wanted no sacrifice or cereal offering, but you gave me a body. You took no pleasure in burnt offerings and the sacrifices for sin; then I said, 'Here I am! I am coming,' in the scroll of the book it is written of me, to do your will, God."

—Hebrews 10:5-7

Thank you, Lord, for your fidelity to the Father's will. You are the ultimate epiphany of the Father's faithfulness to us. Human and divine fidelity meet in you. You show us the splendor of your own promise to use our limping lives to form us in your faithfulness to uphold eternal designs. Every moment is a gentle invitation to share your response to the Father and his creation.

The Father's will shines forth in the simple field of our everyday duties, our sufferings, joys and encounters. Your Father loved us so much that he gave you to us in the midst of our everyday life to relieve its tediousness. "This is how God loved the world:/ he gave his only Son,/ so that everyone who believes in him may not perish/ but may have eternal life" (Jn 3:16).

19

The Holy Spirit makes us gaze at you with trusting eyes of faith and love. Silence our heart so that it may hear your voice. Fidelity is far more than the fulfillment of daily duties. It raises our human spirit by the Spirit of divine love. We do what we have to do joyously as a liturgy of praise to your presence in all things.

Fidelity bestows a new radiance on simple endeavors. It raises us up from willful performance to serene surrender. It lets us know not merely about you, but to know you, for you call us to believe deeply in you and to follow you faithfully.

You lived the life of a carpenter's son in Nazareth. Let us remember you as the young man down the street, the son of the carpenter and his faithful spouse. If we do not know you in your humility and rejection, we do not really see you as you are. You become the faraway founder of a religion called Christianity. Yet, how infinitely more you are. Only the light of faith discloses the meaning of your life, a life that failed, humanly speaking.

People pity us when we proclaim you, the crucified, to be the Savior of the world. They scorn us when we are not embarrassed to converse with sinners, with those who fail; to mingle with the downtrodden; to defend the oppressed; to distance ourselves from the pulsations of our age. "Do not model your behavior on the contemporary world, but let the renewing of your minds transform you, so that you may discern for yourselves what is the will of God—what is good and acceptable and mature" (Rm 12:2).

If we are ashamed to confess and follow you, you will be ashamed of us. "For if anyone is ashamed of me and of my words, of him the Son of man will be ashamed when he comes in his own glory and in the glory of the Father" (Lk 9:26). Fidelity to you is not following you from afar. Only when we are intimate with you can we be truly faithful to you.

Because of your fidelity, you care about each facet of our life. To convince us of that you freely suffered a cruel death. How we need your pledge in our broken lives, permeated by subtle pride. Ego tells us to save ourselves by cleverness and might. Instead of trusting you, we consent to the gimmicks of self-actualization the world glibly advertises. We put great store in our own attempts instead of acknowledging the necessity of your fidelity. We prefer extraordinary deeds, feelings, words and plans to doing the will of the Father in obscurity. Yet you have warned us:

> "It is not anyone who says to me, 'Lord, Lord,' who will enter the kingdom of Heaven, but the person who does the will of my Father in heaven. When the day comes many will say to me, 'Lord, Lord, did we not prophesy in your name, drive out demons in your name, work many miracles in your name?' Then I shall tell them to their faces: I have never known you; *away from me, all evil doers!*" (Mt 7:21-23).

Fidelity is a gift. The Father bestows that gift on us through the Holy Spirit if he sees in us the form of his Son, his beloved one. Our receptivity for this gift depends on our conversion to the form of Christ hidden in our soul. The gift of fidelity enables us to become a manifestation of the Christ form of life. We are called to mirror God's promise in the plainness of daily endeavors.

Divine faithfulness manifests itself in a rich variety of forms of creation. All disclose infinite fidelity.

"Bless Yahweh, all his works/ in every place where he
rules./ Bless Yahweh, my soul" (Ps 103:22).

Lord, you invite us to enter into your kingdom
through faith, hope and love, through the miracle of a
delicate flower, a shining star. The marvels of creation
keep brain and body going. Our ability to know, to
love, to appreciate, to affirm, to recall, to imagine, to
anticipate—*all* are wonderful manifestations of divine
fidelity.

You ask us, Lord, to welcome the dynamism of
love, joy and peace in our life. Bless our home and
family, our friends and adversaries, our labor and leisure. Keep us aware of the fidelity of the Father in
small and great endeavors. We give you thanks for the
wonder of your grace in all things, for the promises
you keep.

In Still Fidelity

Did you read
about the simple man in Nazareth
down the street
who lived in still fidelity
to the Father's will?
His faithfulness in daily doings?
Eons of divine formation
prepared a human body
to be faithful freely
to eternal designs.
Simple life of Nazareth:
Asking humankind
to amplify its mind,
unwind its willfulness,
its anxious stress,
its hunger for success,
in surrender to the will
of a pervasive mystery,
that makes us be
in still fidelity
to a destiny
that slowly unfolds
when life does not withhold
from the rigors of the journey.

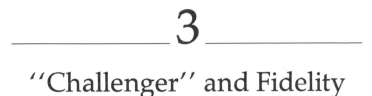

3

"Challenger" and Fidelity

Despite new endeavors in space, many recall with horror the loss of the *Challenger* and its crew. An entire country grieved but did not deny humanity's mission to give form to its destiny by space exploration. In a nationwide poll taken at that time, 80 percent responded that we should go on with the flights. The success of *Discovery* confirmed their faith and proved that the astronauts had not perished in vain. They taught us a lesson in heroic fidelity we will never forget.

Faith of this sort is not foolishness. Those called to space adventure are not only congenial to their individual tasks; they are able, compatible as a team and above all competent. Mechanics, aerospace engineers, trainers and controllers back them up. Their attention to detail is also rooted in a spirit of fidelity. Arrogant indifference or idealistic verbosity never substitutes for faithful growth in competence.

To challenge space is not a sin of hubris. It is an expression of fidelity to the mystery within and without, calling us unceasingly to explore the possibilities of further formation hidden in creation.

As the *Challenger* has shown, fidelity does not exclude risk, danger and death. The fallible human form of life cannot attain the sort of perfection that would make failure unthinkable. The image of *Challenger's* explosion in the sky is etched in our mind. It teaches us that fidelity to any task exposes our vulnerability. We have to pay the price for fidelity and for the new vistas it opens up to us.

Fidelity to the struggle for social justice and cultural transformation, for peace and freedom, for the conquest of disease and discrimination, for trying out new possibilities, has always implied sacrifice of certainties, of energies, of easy popularity, of health, even of lives at times.

Fidelity is not possible if we remain shallow and self-centered. There is no growth without growing pains, no victory without tragedy, no innovation without detraction by those who fear what is new or demanding. The way of fidelity can become a way of fire at any moment. We cannot overcome the injustice of our age, the frightening prospect of nuclear annihilation or environmental contamination and destruction without paying the price the Spirit inspires. Fidelity is a wager, not a joy ride in the night.

Fidelity of people like the astronauts brings them close to the edge of life. The daily grind exposes us less conspicuously. Yet our fidelity too implies loss of life, if not at once in a fiery flash, then over a lifetime of trying. To be faithful as parents in a family, as workers on the job, as teachers, mill hands, writers, artists, athletes or thinkers makes us pay out our life in little pennies day by day, hour by hour.

This is perhaps one of the reasons for the horror we felt over the loss of Christa McAuliffe. She shared with us the grind of daily fidelity in a family, in an everyday job. She paid her dues to fidelity in the common way we all share. This flight was only to be a brief intermezzo. Then she would return to the daily round with which we too can identify. Everything turned out differently. Her death is not in vain if it reminds us that we have to pay a price for fidelity, if not in disaster then in the trenches of everyday-ness.

All who enter the orbit of the Spirit must take the risk of suffering defeats, though we may occasionally find success along the way. Only in the long run may fidelity lead to harmony with the mystery during periods of real peace. We may stray from the faithful life. Thank goodness the trans-human mystery within is always present, issuing an invitation to renewed fidelity. Our refusal can never negate the presence of this transformative power in our life. We can choose not to follow the lead of graced fidelity to our providential tasks, but we cannot hamper the call.

Fidelity: Key to Constancy

Our minds are shaken
by lives that were taken,
by the burning out
of astronauts.
Fireball in the sky
that made us ask: why
stay faithful to a task
that challenges the mask
of complacency,
delaying the discovery
of a mystery within,
a silent spring,
a potency
that makes us be
in a new and daring way,
not allowing us to stay
motionless, without aspiration?
Is ours the dedication
of faithful lives
in contemplation?
Are we decimated
in beehives
of wild activity?
Fidelity is the key
to constancy
in lands of infidelity.

4

Fidelity to Prayer

Thank you, Lord, for your appearance in our history. Your epiphany in Bethlehem is the event of events, the birth of births. Through us you want to illumine our family and community, our places of leisure and labor. What you ask of us is fidelity to your epiphany, your presence at the heart of everyday reality.

The path to epiphany is the path of prayer. The faithful heart finds in itself a mysterious longing for the presence of the Divine. A seed of unceasing prayer is planted in us by the Holy Spirit. To live in fidelity to this longing, we must abide with it, attentive to its invitation. Silent abiding is the beginning of fidelity. The gift of holy longing is veiled for us by anxious concerns, vexing problems, tedious tasks and ambitious pursuits. How large they loom in daily life! How they compel our instant attention! They tear us apart. Our life is like a dish that is broken.

The church as herald and servant communicates to us pathways of fidelity. It is the primary continuation of the divine epiphany in space and time. The needs and pains, the tediousness and struggles of daily liv-

29

ing, may lose their piercing edge during our hours of togetherness in the holy places in which the church makes itself visible for us in its liturgy and ministry of the word.

The life of prayer is as necessary to the life of faith as food and drink, rest and medicine, as breath itself is for our body. Prayer is the soul of fidelity, fidelity the fruit of a prayerful life. Prayer, nourished by scripture and tradition, comes to fruition in charity and justice wherever we live and labor. Fidelity to prayer does not detract us from service. On the contrary, it inspires us to greater dedication, firmer engagement, more self-less motivation. It makes us available to what we are called to do wherever providence has placed us.

Fidelity to prayer is not a luxury but a necessity, not a hobby but a life-saving disposition, not an oddity but a sign of sanity, not a passing interest but a constant nourishment. It is not forced upon us. We are enabled by grace to choose it freely. To live in fidelity to this invitation is not easy, at least not initially. Fidelity to prayer will not evolve without discipline, without periods of recollection and reflection. Many advertisements, educational tools and media productions do not create a climate of fidelity. They focus our attention on fleeting things. They distract us from our presence to the epiphany of God in our life; yet it is the only thing that ultimately matters. Within this world of distraction, we have to give form to a life of prayer so that fidelity may bloom again.

Helpful in this regard is the formation of small groups of people with the same longing. They are called to keep the concern for prayer alive among one another. Together they weave an atmosphere of presence to God in this broken world. They maintain the art of prayer in the midst of a humanity that forgets its necessity.

Fidelity to God's epiphanies is not easily maintained. It is first of all a gift of God to be received in humility. It is not talent, learning, education, success, charm, or ease with words that forms us or others in fidelity. No one alone can evoke presence to the Holy. It is pure grace. It cannot be compelled by human power. It is generously given to those who wait upon it with compunction of heart.

Only the Spirit can spark the thoughts, words and feelings that awaken the life of prayer. The Holy Spirit longs to help us to be humble and gentle, simple and peaceful without affectation. Peace and simplicity facilitate fidelity to the wonder of God's presence among us and the depth of our call to be prayerfully present to God in daily life.

A moment of recollection can be blessed by the divine presence if we leave it more peacefully than when we entered it, if we are more, God-directed than self-directed, more gentle than turbulent, a little wiser than before, more abandoned to Providence, less anxious, less filled with an egocentric need for control. The question is: Are we convinced that the art of presence is the greatest gift we may receive in life? Are we willing to make any sacrifice that may facilitate its reception?

Many people in the world hunger for a life of prayer. They may believe it is only possible for priests, ministers, monks, sisters and brothers. This is as foolish as believing that eating bread is only for bakers, drinking coffee for planters, breathing healthily for doctors, exercise for athletes, reading books for writers. Nothing is more paralyzing to a life of prayer than the idea that it is not possible for us. Our life is far less bountiful than it could be were it nourished by relaxed presence to God in prayer.

The Music of Eternity

Blessedness of Bethlehem,
birth of births, tender stem
of oneness with Eternal Word
that has restored
to renaissance what was decay:
We went astray, we fade away,
the hubris of a fallen race,
the hurried pace,
the idle wish,
the crystal dish
of kindness sadly broken.
Grant us a token
of fidelity in agony.
Steer strife for joy
beyond decoy
of fleeting pleasure
to a treasure
of still abiding
with the tiding
of a lasting melody,
the music of eternity.

5

Jesus' Fidelity: Our Salvation

Like many other people, I wanted to be better than I was. Yet the more I tried, the more I found I could not do it by myself. God made me realize that I could only do it with him. Even with God, the slowness of my improvement kept me down, often low in spirit.

For years I did not quite grasp what Jesus meant when he told us to trust the Holy, to be carefree as birds in the sky, lilies in the field. I did not feel that fidelity was what really counted—not my meager attempts at sanctity. Finally I understood it was not so much my own fidelity but the fidelity of Jesus in me that could save me.

He warned us against clinging to our own virtuousness in self-confidence. He berated the Pharisees for the pride of their piety. He told those who would listen the story of the one in the Temple who boasted of his righteousness, who thanked God that he was not as others were—certainly not like the sinner standing there, as a broken tree in the sanctuary, begging to be healed.

Complacency makes us fools in the eyes of God. If

he lets us see through our pretenses, we begin to sense what is needed to live with Jesus—not spectacular success in self-improvement, but fidelity to the little way of falling down and standing up, of failing and trying again. Over and over we must be the small coin of the gospel story, lost and found by an overjoyed Jesus, symbolized by the housewife who cleansed her whole cottage to retrieve a penny, who called her neighbors to rejoice with her when it was found.

Fidelity must be a sharing in God's own faithfulness to us. His love always outdoes ours. It is the source of our own faint-hearted faithfulness. Jesus is an oasis in the desert of our failures. Each manifestation of his care is a renewal of courage when we have lost hope for the umpteenth time. The faithfulness of Jesus can never fail us. Such is the overwhelming truth of redemption.

Time after time I forgot about being kind to those who envied me, who told stories about me behind my back, of being honest with those who lied to me and used me. I would plunge back into my own world of creature comforts and small concerns. I abdicated the wear and tear of daily faithfulness in common things. To my rude awakening, I found that giving up the path of fidelity meant losing my home in the loyal presence of Jesus.

A comfortable life outside shared loyalty with him becomes a bore. Sharing, no matter how little, in the faithfulness of Jesus is sharing in his loving participation in the Father's will. It is to be lifted up with him into the fire of God's eternal love, mirrored in the immense loyalty of Jesus.

Without a little wisp of fidelity simmering within, life can become distasteful enough to make a marriage come crashing down, to send men and women through foolish pursuits of power, gambling, promiscuity and exotic interludes, to a feverish chase after fantasized heights through dangerous drugs. Nothing of this can heal the tediousness of a life lived outside simple loyalty to a daily task. No human banality can substitute for the balm of fidelity.

To escape the dullness of life, we may dive into the endless seas of stimulation engulfing us from newspapers, TV, billboards, magazines, books, radios, record players, cinemas, tape recorders. Waves of the media beckon us to submerge ourselves in greedy seeing, hearing, reading, sensing, remembering and imagining. We are lured to lose ourselves in streams of news without end, steadily tempted to go beyond what is good for us to experience and do.

It is as if we are balancing on the edge of a dam between swirling waters. Bored by the triteness of simple faithfulness to the everyday, we fall off, almost drown. When God dredges us up again, when he puts us on the still, small path of fidelity, we realize that we only found emptiness where we expected salvation, disappointment where we anticipated fulfillment.

A certain amount of knowledge is good for us. So is entertainment and information; but it must fit into God's loving plan for our life. Fidelity is the buoy that can save us from drowning in the world's confusion and distraction. It is there because Jesus is always there. He is the Good Shepherd who leaves the ninety-nine behind to seek tenderly for the one that is lost. Faithfulness of people to us is sometimes fickle. God's fidelity alone can be trusted always.

Parents, teachers, friends, spouses, children and colleagues may and do radiate to us something of God's own trust, yet even the finest expressions of human loyalty cannot compare to Jesus' which is certain all the time and everywhere.

Many people put their trust in a family, home or

country, in an army, company, bank, union or club, in a team, a hospital, a pension plan. Yet none can compare with the trustworthiness of Jesus. Families can be torn apart; homes washed away; neighborhoods broken up in squabbles; countries devastated by war, terrorism or economic collapse. Armies may lose battles; banks can become insolvent; companies wiped out. Land may be lost in debt, ruined by inundations, earthquakes, storms; hospitals may close by default or be compelled to overprice their services.

The fidelity of Jesus alone is a steadfast rock in the midst of misery. Not for nothing is Yahweh celebrated in the songs of scripture as a faithful God, as firm as granite in a storm.

Few among us may be called to fidelity to some exceptional performance in the history of human formation: to make a breakthrough in medicine, to compose symphonies that ennoble the spirit, to sing songs that warm the heart of the multitudes, to create a stirring novel or a lovely ballet, a fine scientific theory, to administer wisely a state, a country, a school, a company.

We must encourage such gifted persons to move uniquely with the music of eternal love. For them too, however, it will only be the tedious string of small fidelities in the midst of envy, adversity, gossip and ridicule that may bring about the victory of ultimate fidelity. Some of them may imagine that celebrity is sheer satisfaction. Others feel more like the reluctant prophets of the Old Testament. They would prefer to hide from the crowds in blessed forgetfulness. Be that as it may, in the end their achievement like ours will depend on everyday struggles with bothersome details.

The fidelity of Jesus to us is often the only source of our faint smile in the midst of pain, opposition and defeat. For his fidelity alone keeps us believing that even a miserable life is meaningful. It kindles the hope that our small limping fidelity will be transformed into an eternal loving gaze upon the Trinity in ceaseless fidelity of the Eternal Son in whom we live and move and have our being.

———————————

Thank you, Lord, for being our fidelity with the Father. Help us not to sell ourselves short, remind us how unspeakably worthwhile each of us is in the eternal embrace of the Trinity.

Still Delight in Daily Duties

I

I feel low in spirit, Lord.
Whisper a word
of fidelity
that generates serenity
in my uncertain heart.
Make me the ward
of your wish
to save my limping life.

II

My trust should be bold,
you told prophets of old,
people of Galilee,
fishers in the boat
that crossed the sea,
throwing out a net
in trust of you, instead
of in their skill alone.

III

Please raise my home
on the mountain of fidelity
that holds humanity,
the dawning of its day,
the passing of each century.
Set me free as a bird in the sky,
a lily that blooms without why,

a wounded tree daily healed
by fidelity that yields
fruits from starving branches.

IV

Your love dances through dissonances
of hearts that faint in pain,
reviving once again
a still delight in daily duties
no longer meaningless and vain.

V

For I am the coin
lost and found by you alone,
eternal seeker, ever trailing
high or deep the wailing sheep,
guiding each one tenderly
through the gate of your fidelity.

6

Mosaic of Victory

Fidelity is a two-way street: God's fidelity to me, mine to God.

Trust in the divine promise helps me to solve my problem just as it has helped countless others to do the same. If I live in this trust, I may expect wonderful changes to occur in my life. I may experience inner healing. Fidelity is more healing than anything else. In trusting God's love, I let go of hurt. I sense the presence of God's promise in my life. Past sorrows fade away. Instead of keeping my wounds open, I choose to let what has happened teach me to use yesterday for my unfolding tomorrow.

The more I practice letting go, the more I can release painful memories. Jesus wants to give a unique form to my life through all of these happenings. I ask him for the grace to appreciate and affirm what he wants me to become. I begin to feel good about who he calls me to be.

Lord, you want me to develop a disposition of quiet attentiveness to the expressions of your fidelity to me, great and small: the bread on my table, the rose

41

in my garden, the smile of a child, the delight of the sun warming my face, the freshness of dew and rain, the magic of a kind word from someone I love. I appreciate more and more your eternal love shining forth in simple things. My heart sings the antiphon of the Holy Office: "The Lord is faithful in all his words and loving in all his deeds."

The creative fidelity of the Mystery stretches like luminous skin over my surroundings. The stream of divine fidelity guides my own good and the good of others. On my part, I need to be attentive to the Spirit's urgings within. If they are in consonance with scripture and tradition and with the demands of my life, I can follow them confidently.

At times I may feel that my life is not worth much. Discard such sentiments. They are temptations, smoke screens arising from despondent fantasies. They are not from the Spirit.

No life is worthless in God's vision. I am totally loved by God. My life is called to be one with God. Wholeheartedly I embrace this truth in gratefulness. I cherish this gem of beauty. It shores up my shaky self-appreciation. Why would I ever doubt the fidelity of divine love?

Life may seem dispersed in little pieces. At times they all bore me to tears. I cannot see the wonderful unity only beheld by the eyes of faith.

The hidden harmony of my destiny may be masked by incidents that seem unconnected. Yet God's promise of love connects everything in time and eternity. He brings my dispersed life, with its ups and downs, to a glorious end. His fidelity turns my small and painful passage through time into a splendid mosaic of victory in the face of defeat, a victory strikingly portrayed in the death and resurrection of Jesus!

If we lack trust in divine fidelity, it is difficult to believe that defeat can conceal victory, that the effect of anger, envy and hostility can be transformed into benefits beyond telling. Jesus' story keeps illuminating the shadows of my day. His life fills my night with brightness.

Such trust is not a magic wand. We cannot wave it and expect to fulfill every idle wish. Life does not work that way.

To gain the benefits of God's fidelity, we must respond with our own. His gift is there for the taking, but we are free to accept or reject it. God wants us to grow in faithfulness to his directives for good and wise living. God planted them in our hearts and reveals them further in his words. They are to be put into practice freely and joyfully. Then we may find out how they work.

To apply these directives, not only to read about them, is a challenge to fidelity. All events in our life are meant as opportunities to unfold the grace given uniquely to us. The problems we face are Jesus' way of shaking us up and saying again: "Here is another opportunity to grow in trust, to learn how to appreciate others, to give birth to ideas, to serve humanity." Jesus uses encounters and all kinds of situations to teach us in the school of faithful attentiveness.

I met a young woman who lived with this kind of faith. She awoke one morning with an inspiration, as if from the Lord, informing her: "You are single, my dear. I gave you lots of time not only for yourself but also to minister to others. I did not grant you this call to the single life just to enjoy your freedom in leisure without care for a family of your own." This thought sent her mind spinning. She conceived the idea of

studying spirituality so that later on she might be able
to communicate insights to other people in a way that
would be meaningful to them. Faithful to this inspiration and the ideas it generated, she took many
courses in this field. Her aim was not to succeed *per se*
but to serve. God has used her to move many people
to a deeper spiritual life by means of lecturing and
writing.

Others have found different inspirations in keeping with their own time, talents and energies. Some
are inspired to feed the hungry, to visit the sick, to volunteer for parish work. Others drive handicapped
neighbors to physicians, stores or schools. They find
outlets for loving service, no matter how insignificant
they may be.

A higher power of divine fidelity dwells in and
around us. We have only to plug into it, as it were, by
faithful attention to its inspirations. To keep this attentiveness alive we should often take "fidelity breaks,"
moments of silent meditation, of becoming still, of allowing the providence of God to have its way with us.

In the beginning the atmosphere of trusting fidelity will often be disturbed by feelings of anxiety, irritation, annoyance. What then? To distance ourselves
from them is the first step. We must not allow ourselves to be overcome by them. Instead say: "I am
more than these disturbances. I am more than my
worry or anger, my being upset. I need not drown in
this swamp of bad feelings."

God granted a marvelous dimension to my life, my
human spirit. Jesus enriched and deepened it with his
Holy Spirit. It is the still-point of my soul. The more I
make my home in this part of me, the more I may learn
to manage disturbing sentiments. They may be there,
but they will be less overwhelming.

As I feel myself becoming more calm, I can bask in

the light of God's faithful love shining softly in my spirit.

The next step is to discern if there is something in what happened to me that can be appreciated as good, that offers me an opportunity to grow in wisdom, patience, forbearance and effective action. Afterwards I recollect myself again in the still-point of my soul. There the Spirit of Jesus may flood me with faith, hope and love. Illumined now is the possible goodness of painful events. God gives me the grace to dwell on them as appreciable. He enables me to discover diamonds of beauty in the dullness of suffering.

Indwelling Fidelity

Indwelling Fidelity
that penetrates and carries me
with all created things,
that loves and links
all things in harmony
in interweaving history.

Don't delay the gracious dance
by mindless arrogance,
by drive for dominance
of splinters of creation
deforming things in our image, Lord,
instead of celebrating a Word
that still ascends
within all things
towards an end
that transcends
the musings of humanity.

Do not demean the cosmic
dreams of divinity
by reams of facts and figures,
strictures on streams of sympathy
with God's emergent symphony.

7

Trust in God's Fidelity

Trust implies an appreciation of God's gifts in our life as manifestations of his fidelity. The power of trust is immense.

An acquaintance of mine suffered from alcoholism. The disease destroyed his life and the happiness of his family. He joined Alcoholics Anonymous. With others, he reflected on the AA maxim that only a Higher Power can help one to overcome addiction. Meditation on this fact opened him to trust in divine fidelity. He experienced the beginning of a deeper spiritual life. Slowly, he became liberated from his addiction.

In the same way we too can put our trust in God. We too can be in touch with a Higher Power. The key is to renew our trust in God's fidelity to us. Trust in God's faithfulness enables us to affirm his will for us. We must not be satisfied with only renewing this affirmation now and then. God calls us to renewal continuously. Doing so we develop a lasting disposition of affirmation. It is available to us every moment the need for it arises. Trusting affirmation helps us to diminish the impact of unpleasant happenings on our thoughts, moods, feelings and actions. Do not wait to start your daily training in affirmative thinking and the appreciative outlook on life that goes with it. Otherwise, when a crisis happens, you may not be ready for it.

To turn appreciation and affirmation into an effective force, you must work at it daily. Here are a few suggestions. Try in the midst of everyday challenges to trust God thoroughly. In every unpleasant thing something can be found to be appreciated in faith. Train yourself in bringing up appreciative thoughts and feelings as a response to disappointments, little resistances of people and things, unpleasant news, tiny discomforts, pinpricks of contradictions, slight condemnations. Become aware of the beginnings of depreciative reactions during times of trial. See these moments as opportunities for growth in faith, wisdom and fidelity. Fill mind and heart with silent affirmations of God's fidelity in the midst of unpleasantness. Do the same at night before sleep. Create "fidelity breaks" during the day to dwell on God's promise never to leave us orphaned.

Some may choose a special text for this purpose or make one up for all occasions such as, "Your fidelity keeps me confident and competent at all times today, no matter what difficulties may come my way." Such affirmations make us aware of the resources of grace God grants to us.

Another inner step forward involves using our imagination for spiritual growth. Anticipate in your imagination that you have to cope with something that might get you down or upset. Try to imagine the upcoming situation as vividly as possible. Review it carefully in your mind. Remind yourself that you have overcome difficulties before by trusting in the Lord's fidelity. Ask yourself how you can do so during the upcoming trial. Deepen in memory, imagination and anticipation the conviction that you can survive almost anything with God's help. If faith can move mountains, it surely can take care of the molehills we stumble over.

During "fidelity breaks" imagine how you want yourself to appear and act in a tight situation that is facing you. Then, when you are imaginatively inserted in that situation, let affirmation of God's fidelity come to your aid. This will be easier when you develop a disposition of trust. You may then find yourself reacting spontaneously in the right way.

You feel confident and competent because of God's promise. "True to your word, support me and I shall live; do not disappoint me of my hope" (Ps 119:116). Faith in divine fidelity sustains our rocky life. It is like a mighty aircraft carrier in the midst of the turbulent ocean of this world. It makes us feel at ease in spite of everything to the contrary.

Our at-homeness in God's fidelity may give others a feeling of at-homeness too. Our life can become a mirror of the "more than." God may use us as a means to make others aware of his promise in their lives too. They discover the hidden treasure of trust in God.

People easily lose contact with the stream of fidelity pouring from God through them into their daily life. "Fidelity breaks" may be difficult in mills, factories, offices and schools. It might be helpful if a "quiet room" could be set aside in such places where one could sit for a few moments. The stress of work, telephone calls from colleagues, meetings with administrators becomes too much. How good it would be to retreat for five or ten minutes at least. The results may prove to be more relaxing than a double martini!

To use such "fidelity pauses" well, we should have at hand texts that inspire us. If we have dwelt on them, they may have gained a deeper meaning for us. We can collect them in a small book, like the one in

which we write addresses. Unlike other telephone re-
minders, these connect us not with other people but
with the mystery of the divine presence. Inspiring
texts may ward off any boredom we feel when sitting
in a quiet room. They help us to bore deeper, to dive
under the maelstrom of worries and distractions that
may surge up the moment we find ourselves alone in
silent surroundings.

You may say, "I can see that I can dwell on God's
fidelity in a meditation room. But how do I do it when I
get upset or impatient in my busy day? People can be
so irritating; daily duties can be so distracting!"

At such occasions you can ask yourself, on the spot
or shortly after: "What irritates me, makes me lose patience?" Asking this you say in fact, "It is not all of me
that is annoyed. For in that case there would be nothing left in me that could ask the question. There must
be some higher part of me that can still go beyond irritation."

That part is my graced spirit. God's healing fidelity
announces itself in my spirit all the time through his
Holy Spirit. I must learn to look at my agitation from
the viewpoint of trust in his faithfulness. The Holy
Spirit enables me to grow in this trust. All things that
happen are meant for my growth. Trust in God enables me to look for any possibility for improvement. I
believe that opportunities are hidden in events that
upset me. I become aware that I can do something
about the situation.

God granted each of us the power of choice. Therefore, we can say, "With your help, Lord, I hope to
make the situation better. Please make me see openings for improvement. Enable me to picture in my
mind as vividly as possible how I can go about using
every opportunity you offer, trusting in your guid-
ance."

We see such trust in the stories of Anne Frank as depicted in her *Diary of a Young Girl* and of Etty Hillesum in her book, *An Interrupted Life*. Both died in concentration camps. These young Jewish women experienced persecution before being transported to their cruel date with death. Yet they were able to grow in the Spirit, to cope with the turn in the history that took their lives. They had a choice: to drown in despondency or to trust that even in this deadly interruption they could do something appreciative; they could turn despair into hope on the wings of grace.

Faithfulness to God's design implies that we take responsibility for our lives no matter how drab or painful they turn out to be. We stop making excuses. We go to work. We imagine practically the better life we want, the life to which God calls us.

At night we put into our imagination the videocassette of the day's happenings. We try to look at them with God's eyes. We see clearly where and how we were not faithful to our calling. This replay discloses to us how we acted in disgraceful ways. Perhaps we lived unwittingly in envy. We have to admit that we behaved meanly and competitively. We profited from other people. They were seduced by our pleasantness to cater to our whims.

Now is the time to ask the Lord to make us aware of how we can do better when similar situations occur. We must engage ourselves in imaginary reformations repeatedly. This exercise will engrave a new "groove" in the record of our memory. Then when we are faced with a similar event, the record of our responses will play a wiser tune rooted in the groove of trust in divine fidelity. Then we can say with the psalmist: "I hate a divided heart,/ I love your Law./ You are my refuge and shield,/ I put my hope in your word" (Ps 119:113-114).

Videocassette of a Dreadful Day

Let me replay tonight
in the light
of your fidelity
the videocassette
of my dreadful day:
my drift away
from your embrace,
my loss of gentle pace
my small appreciation
of divine origination
of each event that bends
my life to wider ends.

This day I went the other way,
You had no say:
I turned away
from your hand
to the land
of defeats,
the dead-end streets
of trusting myself alone
losing my home
in your faithfulness,
living less
in hope of things to come.
I was deaf and dumb.
Enable my imagination

to ready me for the temptation
to repeat my defeat
this coming day.

Let me foresee
how I may stray.
Give me the key
to reformation
of irritation
that carries me
to a betrayal
of the transformation
you want for me.

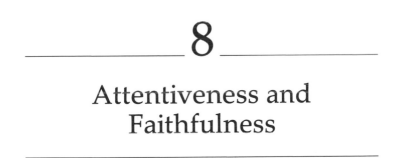

8

Attentiveness and Faithfulness

Pay attention to your daily doings. This will advance your faithfulness. Caring for the children, doing the dishes well, cleaning the house, making the beds with care, driving to work cautiously—all can be done in fidelity to God's presence if you do it with and for him. It can increase your power to attend to anything at all.

Attentiveness is a condition for faithfulness to the divine call. God's call permeates our life in its myriad details. Therefore, daily demands can be seen as invitations from the Trinity to practice fidelity.

Being attentive in this way is a celebration of the sacrament of the present moment. It implies increased attentiveness to the sacred aspect of what we see, hear and do—attendance to a presence that can only grow over a lifetime.

Attention to the whispers of grace requires that we do not let agitation dominate our mind and heart. We cannot be attentive to others or to our task when we are absorbed in worries and fantasies. Hunger for success may mean that we do not trust fully.

Trying to be attentive, we may find that our mind

runs in circles. A mother told her daughter, "I'll buy you a new dress if you do the dishes with full attention, thinking and talking about nothing else." How easy, thought the girl. She started cleaning pots and pans. Suddenly, she stopped: "Will the dress have lace on top?" Full attention is easy to promise, difficult to achieve.

Fidelity in daily doings deepens relaxed presence to the task at hand. We focus our mind on what the Spirit asks us to do. Our commitment to daily demands is firmer when we realize that they are an expression of God's will for us. To be really effective, we have to learn the art of sustained attention even if we do not succeed at first. Enthusiastic feelings of the moment cannot make up for the quiet consistency of persistent attention.

We may think that commitment to small affairs has little to do with our life of prayer. The opposite is true. First of all, fidelity to daily duties—if we see them as opportunities for intimacy with God—is already a prayer of practical union with him. To keep this union alive we should set apart certain moments of the day for nothing other than prayer and spiritual reading. These practices can be done well only if we pay full attention. When our prayer is deep enough, our attention may be turned by grace toward God alone and his word.

Many tasks that make up our day call for a lesser kind of attention than prayer and meditation. Still, simple attention to details of everyday life helps us to be more attentive to the other, more difficult things we have to do. We should direct our attention not only to the details of our work but also to the "will of God" that underlies our daily tasks. Soon we shall find that our improved power of attentiveness will be available to us during prayer and spiritual reading.

Chores can thus be challenges from the Most High. God asks us to be attentive to his will hidden in the burdens and blessings of any day. All are welcomed as chances to train our wandering attention. Doing things with care prepares us to attend to God fully at moments of recollection.

Once, on a foreign mission journey, I met a young person who had volunteered as a nurse in a mission hospital for lepers. I asked her if she liked what she was doing. She answered, "Liking is not the right word. I am just beginning here. I feel appalled by the dirt, stench and disfiguration of the patients they carry in from the bush. Often I feel like running away. But I stay for the love of God; I try to see Christ in their fractured bodies. This helps me to honor them with full attention in the midst of filth, groans, despair and death. In this sense, yes, I love my work, but I cannot as yet say I like it."

Loving and liking are not the same. Loving is a decision of our free will but liking people and our work for them is not always in our power.

It was difficult for this nurse to be wholly present to patients while distracted and repelled by their sad condition. She wrestled with aversion so that it would not get the best of her and paralyze her caring presence to them. She went through a tough school of learning that no college or university could offer. What did she learn? To be attentive in spite of distractions, dislikes and repulsions. Because she did so with an eye on Christ, her efforts were not in vain. She may not have succeeded fully in this situation. Yet she was surprised by her new-found power of attentiveness. It had grown in her during the struggle against the temptation to escape depressing situations. She had turned her distaste into an advantage, an opportunity for growth. She may not have been able to overcome her aversion. What counts is that she tried not to give in to it.

Often we fail in our efforts. Efforts that may seem useless can prove useful in a higher way. For one thing they show God that we are people of good will. Our lack of success helps to keep us humble and patient. Fidelity to caring attentiveness in the midst of failure does bear fruit. It fosters growth in attentiveness both in prayer and in other areas of life where obstacles are less steep for us.

How do we develop our power of attention? Attention means that we put not only our minds but also our hearts in whatever we are doing. If a mother is attentive to her children, she knows what they look like, do and say. Attention to a story makes us concentrate on the meaning of the sentences we read. If a missioner strives to be attentive to the needs of the poor, he better understands their plight.

It is not enough to pretend that we look with our eyes or listen with our ears. We may go to church without conviction. When a preacher appears in the pulpit, we feel obliged to honor him with a show of attention. We may also do it to avoid the bemused glances of people in our pew if we dare to fall asleep. In spite of our lack of interest, we pretend to pay attention to what the preacher has to say.

In this case our attention is more an example of willful contraction than of quiet concentration. If we really care, attention comes naturally. The loving mother, the avid baseball fan, the seasoned archaeologist, the committed physician, the graced contemplative do not have to force themselves to be attentive to children, baseball matches, archaeological findings, symptoms of illness, or God's presence. They are spontaneously attentive, for they have found joy in the things they learn or do. Their hearts are in it.

We feel joy in giving attention to what delights us. We should look also for hidden divine invitations to fidelity. Then we add to our practical attention a higher spiritual attention rooted in the desire to be faithful to God's love. Such higher aspirations cannot be evoked by our own powers alone. They are a gift of Christ who dwells in us. He makes us share in his own faithfulness to the Father's will, in his longing to follow it in his life, no matter what.

Committed Christians thus strive to grow in two kinds of attention: to their responsibilities in daily life and to the manifestations of God's will in these responsibilities. These two kinds of attention do not exclude one another. Our attention to daily responsibilities develops our overall power of paying attention. Grace takes up this improved attention. It elevates it into an attentiveness to God.

Conversely, if we give attention to the spiritual meanings of our chores, we will also pay more attention to their practical details. This makes us more concerned about our daily duties. We want to glorify the Father by doing them as well as we can. They become for us sacraments of practical union with God in the midst of our busy day.

People like cab drivers, mailmen, coal miners, teachers, waitresses, housewives or social workers may express their fidelity to God's glory in doing their task well. They do it with more care than they might have done without this inspiration. Blessed be the country, the company, the school, the family, the church where people meet and work in attentiveness to God's presence in everything they do!

Your Presence Is a Sacrament

Attentiveness and faithfulness
feed and bless
the caring life:
To be best, to dive
in the well
of things, events,
to dwell in the will
that pure and still
deepens all
with a call
to meet the Lord
not only in word
but in the daily drain . . .
that he may reign
in what we suffer, say,
in strain and play.
Your presence is a sacrament
imbuing each event
designed by you attentively
as advents of fidelity.

9

Fidelity and Immortality

It is not easy for us to live in fidelity when we are besieged by the burdens of life. Striking examples of
abandonment in horrendous situations inspire us to
carry on with courage. Etty Hillesum, a modern Jewish woman who lived in Amsterdam during the Nazi
occupation, writes in her diary that her life was interrupted not only by the indignities she suffered at the
hands of the Nazis but by the advent of God's grace.
Up to that time her life had been lived without God,
without faith. Her diary and her letters are a testimony
to heroic fidelity.

Etty was 27 years old when she began writing in
her journal. It was March, 1941, in Amsterdam. She
composed a remarkable record of the miracle of grace
and fidelity she experienced in the midst of imprison-
ment and the threat of annihilation. She was truly surprised by grace. She found herself unaccountably on
her knees before God when she could not go out into
the street because of her Jewishness. This moment
marked the end of her lack of faith, the beginning of a
love story with the Eternal. Fidelity to this grace made
her volunteer as a "social worker" for the concentration camp in spite of the fact that her post in the Jewish

Council in Amsterdam exempted her initially from internment. Fidelity to grace kept her radiant in the midst of mud and misery, sickness, noise and fear. She witnessed the remorseless rhythm of deportations to Auschwitz of thousands of horrified women, men and children whom she tried to encourage by caring words and unsparing service.

Survivors still remember her "shining personality." Buoyed by her newly experienced presence of the Mystery in her heart, she could not resist writing again and again, "Despite everything, life is full of beauty and meaning." Fidelity to God and his people made her spurn attempts by friends to hide her in a safe place during the period in which this would have been possible before final internment in Westerbork, the Dutch camp of transition, to be followed by deportation to Auschwitz. Etty was faithful to the last moment. A friend described her departure on the cattle train toward certain death in Auschwitz: "Talking gaily, smiling, a kind word for everyone she met on the way, full of sparkling humor, perhaps just a touch of sadness, but every inch the Etty you all know so well . . ." (Etty Hillesum, *Letters from Westerbork*, New York, Pantheon Books, 1986, p. xvi).

This woman of valiant faith threw a postcard out of the moving death train that said: "We left the camp singing" (p. 146). How moving are the words of grateful fidelity, written by her at Westerbork on August 18, 1943:

> You have made me so rich, O God, please let me share out your beauty with open hands. My life has become an uninterrupted dialogue with You, O God, one great dialogue. Sometimes when I stand in some corner of the camp, my feet planted on Your earth, my

eyes raised toward Your heaven, tears
sometimes run down my face, tears of deep
emotion and gratitude. At night too, when I
lie in my bed and rest in You, O God, tears of
gratitude run down my face, and that is my
prayer. I have been terribly tired for several
days, but that, too, will pass. Things come
and go in a deeper rhythm, and people must
be taught to listen: it is the most important
thing we have to learn in this life. I am not
challenging you, O God, my life is one great
dialogue with You. I may never become the
great artist I would really like to be, but I am
already secure in You, God. Sometimes I try
my hand at turning out small profundities
and uncertain short stories, but I always end
up with just one single word: God. And that
says everything and there is no need for anything more. And all my creative powers are
translated into inner dialogues with You.
The beat of my heart has grown deeper,
more active, and yet more peaceful, and it is
as if I were all the time storing up inner
riches (p. 116).

This woman, "already secure in You, God," who
"left the camp singing" to travel to what she knew
would be her death, must have had a taste of immortality. This enabled Etty to be an epiphany, an appearance of God's goodness, in the forbidding barracks
about which she writes. "At night the barracks sometimes lay in the moonlight, made out of silver and eternity; like a plaything that had slipped from God's pre-
occupied hand" (p. 100).

Something tells her that life is not an idle day-
dream, an empty wish, a forlorn hope. She feels embraced by an eternal Love with whom she lives in daily
conversation. In the hidden depth of her life, ap-

proaching death was but a turnstile to a larger exist-
ence. She was not lost in the maze of sufferings
heaped upon her and her fellow victims in the camp.
She refused to become blinded to the splendor of the
rising life within her. In the midst of a place of sad despondency, the Mystery glows in what she calls the
"thinking heart of the barracks" God wants her to be.

She appreciates every event as an opportunity to
rise to a "life . . . full of beauty and meaning" (p. xi).
She lives and dies in praise of a presence that lets her
taste immortality even if she does not express that miracle in words and concepts. For, in regard to the deepest experiences, concepts conceal more than they clar-
ify.

The words of revelation bring us nearer to the rising of the life for which we are longing. For Christians
Jesus is the ultimate epiphany of the Mystery. He
brightens the history of humanity by his resurrection
from death. A life of Christian fidelity is a daily imple-
mentation of his rising for and with us. Fidelity is celebrating the enduring resurrection of Christ in our
lives. Fidelity means to renew daily the faith that we
ourselves in a unique way are called to be an epiphany
of the risen Lord in our families, in the workplace, in
our love for people everywhere.

The tomb, in which Jesus was placed, stands for
everything that looks as though life were buried, paralyzed and lost. It symbolizes despondency, infidelity,
failure, discouragement and disease. But Jesus rose
from the tomb. The crucifixion and the pain, the dread
in the garden, humiliation and defeat, the burial, were
but passing events. All were preparations for the resurrection, the triumph of life, the manifestation of a divine fidelity to our suffering race like the fidelity of divine compassion that flowed freely through the heart
and hands of Etty, the light of Westerbork.

The more we respond in fidelity to God's promise, the more we will awaken from the tomb of fear, worry, resentment, envy, bitterness and anxiety. We are all sinners, but at any moment we can turn to God for forgiveness. Repenting, we are embraced by the Risen One within. He whispers to us what he said to the thief on the cross beside him, "Today you will be with me in paradise" (Lk 23:43).

All that Jesus said and did gives us the assurance that our personal life will exist beyond the grave. His fidelity to his promise is unquestionable. We will not perish but rise to everlasting life. Did not an inner revelation of such immortality sustain the joy of Etty in the concentration camp?

The risen Lord is our life now. Our life itself must become a hymn of praise to Jesus rising in us. At times we are inundated in anxious anticipation of what may happen to us and to the world. But faith tells us that Jesus will triumph. The Christ form in the depth of our being will begin to express itself in glorious transformation.

Jesus tells us that the kingdom of God is at hand in each of us. It is already here and now, for we are called to share his resurrection in humanity and history. Let us no longer carry the burdens of the past into our tomorrows. Let us learn to appreciate each day as one of resurrection and rejoicing. Appreciation is the fruit of appraising all happenings, even the smallest or most painful, as precious occasions for an increase in hope and trust.

The word *appraising* has the word *praise* within it. When we welcome each event as an opportunity to grow in praise of the Lord, we appreciate it in the deepest sense. Because of this link with "praise of the Lord," the words appraisal and appreciation are cherished by people who live in fidelity. These words far

surpass more neutral terms like discernment or positive thinking. Appreciation reminds us more directly
of the risen presence within that sings the eternal
praise of the Father. Daily we renew our life in simple
doings in which we allow God to show himself as he
did in the life of Etty Hillesum during its dramatic clo-
sure.

A Taste of Immortality

Thank you, Lord,
for being faithful to your word
that you would rise again
to lift the lame,
the wounded and the lone,
the ones with hearts of stone
from tombs they made their own.
Fill with risen life
families, children, husband, wife:
a taste of immortality,
the lifting of humanity
to mountains of undying hope
from which they come
with passions, problems, pain.
No longer proud and vain
but praising the epiphany,
the splendor of a Mystery
invading planet earth:

The Spirit and the virgin met
in the little town of Nazareth
to generate a wondrous child
that would rise mighty, mild
to make us whole
by rising in the soul
of the simple and the poor,
of the thinker and the doer,
of the sinner and the innocent;
wherever the Animator went
life was generated,
wounded people celebrated
the gracious epiphany
of eternal Fidelity.

10

The Art of Appreciation

Faith in God's fidelity opens vistas not dreamt of before. It is a rock under our stumbling feet. Faith makes it possible for our thoughts to dwell on the good things God wants for us. Therefore, say to yourself:

I enjoy using the mind God gave to me. I gently watch what I think. What begins in my thoughts takes form in my life. God wants me to dwell on thoughts that can improve my life. Good thoughts will attract good images and feelings. They make it easier to change my life for the better. To be practical, let me imagine concretely in every detail the good things I hope to accomplish. This will create in me an inner readiness for them, an eagerness to do them well in the midst of the obstacles I have already overcome in my imagination. For as I think, feel and imagine, so will I begin to live.

To be faithful to God's call I must not dwell on what is discouraging. That would get me down. Instead I trust in the seeds of courage God planted in me. I nurse them daily. Daily burdens then become bridges to his presence.

At times I feel alone, Lord, a little depressed. Please remind me of your fidelity. Renew my faith that you want to lift me out of worry and despondency. Grant me the grace to remember that you gave me the power to give a new direction to my somber thoughts. Help me to see how I lost that power, how I can get it back again.

Stop my abuse of the mind you gave to me. Let me no longer dwell on things that drag me down. Disclose to me the possibilities for growth you open up in adverse situations.

Make me aware of the bent of my mind. Am I inclined to dwell on the good or the bad side of life? Do I only see grayish clouds or also their silver linings? Only obstacles or also opportunities?

God helps us to purify our thoughts from the shadows of despondency. We can learn to think good thoughts. We can learn to appreciate ourselves and others as persons loved by God. If we begin to live in faithfulness to that belief, our life will change. We will become much happier, more disciplined persons. We will be less despondent, moody or angry, less bitter and resentful, more appreciative of who we are and what others most deeply are. From an appreciative mind good directives for living begin to flow. They radiate into our personality. Sustained by grace they transform us. Through us they enter and brighten our life situation. They lift up the people we meet.

God wants us to appreciate ourselves as special. Every human form of life is unique in his eyes. There is no one in the universe exactly like you or me. He made us into a human form of life that is unrepeatable. He remains faithful to what he has created. He loves it when we try to move with him faithfully and contentedly through our busy days. Therefore say to yourself:

I shall appreciate the people I meet. Each one is loved by God. In each something good is to be found. I shall cherish the little spots of light that sparkle throughout the grayness of a dreary day. Make me abide in appreciation, Lord. Let me

*notice the smallest glitter that appears in the midst of mud
and misery.*
    *Let me find happiness in what I am doing, no matter how
small it may seem. Nothing done in fidelity is insignificant
in your eyes. Everything good has your holy name written in
it. You want me to read each of these names of yours, to
praise and hallow them profoundly. Therefore you taught us
to pray: "Hallowed be thy name" (cf. Mt 6:7-13).*

    God is spirit. We cannot see him directly, but his
name is inscribed in the things he created. He keeps
forming them in countless ways. Hence, every little
thing, every small movement of our mind, our heart,
our hands, should carry about it the aura of worship.
    Suffering will strike, crises will emerge, loss will be
felt, misunderstanding will crucify us. These blows
should be dealt with in fidelity to his love. They will
enable us to emerge stronger than before. God's love
will never let us down, even if we feel undone.
    How different life will be for us when we begin to
realize that God's fidelity does not lie outside of us.
From the beginning it is embedded in the hidden
powers he formed in us. God invites us to be faithful to
this inner gift, to believe in it, to live by it, to use it. But
we must learn to reach within, to find there the graced
directives and the power to let these gifts give form to
our life.
    Yes, God granted us power over our life and our
relationships, even over our vital well-being. With his
grace, we can transform our life by changing our
thinking from what is depreciative to what is appreciative. We can move from doubt to faith, from despondency to hope, from condemnation to love of self and
others, from indifference to involvement. All is possible for those who believe. We can respond to the divine invitation to transformation any time we surren-

der to grace. The choice is ours. Any choice for the
better is an affirmation of our faith in God's fidelity.

Faith, as Jesus said, can move mountains. We
must accept responsibility for our thoughts and the
feelings and images that go with them. Of course, it
takes effort. But if we live in fidelity to the divine
power within us, saying "yes" will grow easier as the
years go by.

Fidelity to the mystery of transformation within us
will open us to the same mystery in those we meet.
Faith will make us see the call to nobility in all who
pass us by. To the eyes of faith the splendor of divine
fidelity lights up in street cleaners and bus drivers, in
bartenders and high-rise dwellers, in the hungry and
destitute, in faceless passersby, in teeming city streets.
All share God's fidelity. All are called to radiate the
"good news" to those who cross their path. Touched
by the Divine, we can give ourselves anew to the tedious tasks we have to perform day after day. We know
that events will now take on new meaning, thanks to
the transforming power of our graced "yes" to God.

A Mystery Within

Vistas open wide
for those who still abide
with the mystery
in you and me.

A mystery within
salutes the mystery in him
who cleans a dirty room
with a decaying broom.
Loving mystery
that pours nobility
in a woman baking bread,
in a girl of Nazareth,
in a boy who cleans a car,
a tender of a bar,
in victims of vicinity:
a woman clinging desperately
to a dying child,
the high-rise growing wild
around her
with violence and pride
of battling gangs.
The hungry in the streets
mingling like weeds
with flowery passersby
who know not the why
of own prosperity
or others' misery.
Make us sense the Mystery
that calls to them
to you and me,
so painfully, so steadily.

11

Conflict and Fidelity

Life without conflict is unthinkable. Conflict itself is not bad. What we do with it is the question. Conflict is not an obstacle; it is an opportunity for fidelity.

Lord, let me not be aggravated by the strain of conflict. Let me embrace it as an occasion to grow with you in fidelity to the Father's will. Prevent me from depreciating this gift. Let your Spirit inspire me to flow with conflict firmly and gently. Your Spirit did this for you too when conflict arose in your life: conflict between love for your parents and love for your mission when you were inspired as a youth to stay behind in the Temple of Jerusalem; conflict renewed in you when you had to leave your widowed mother; conflict in the desert when Satan tempted you; conflict when you were asked to perform a miracle in Cana before your time had come; conflicts with disciples who did not understand, with priests, scribes, Pharisees and Zealots. How much your life was disrupted by conflicts people imposed on you. Thank you, Lord, for teaching me. You used every disruption of your life to express your fidelity to the Father's will, to the mission

that he gave to you. Thank you for calling me to follow
in your footsteps along the way.

Conflict is a source of formation of life, a bright
beacon on our journey. This can be said in some way of
the formation story of the cosmos. God created the
cosmos in such a way that it would unfold through
small or cataclysmic conflicts. Think for a moment
about diamonds dug from the depths of the earth.
They delight us by their shape and sparkle, their
strength and endurance. Yet they were formed from
eons and eons of conflict—of upheavals of the crust of
our planet, of sinking sands, decaying woods and
splintered rocks pressed together for millenia by immense weights above and around them.

Human life is called to give form to diamonds of
fidelity under the pressure of conflicts. The Spirit invites us to widen the reach of the gift of consonance in
us by resolving the conflicts God allows in our life.
Conflicts occur within and without. Within ourselves
we have to cope with the dissonances between our will
and God's, between spirit and body, heart and mind,
between the Holy Spirit and the demonic, between
passion and reason. It is only in the graced transcen-
dence of conflict that inner harmony or peace is regained on a deeper level.

Conflicts emerge in our relationships with those
entrusted to our care as well as with our enemies. No
marriage can grow without conflict, no friendship can
keep alive and no community can mature without
growth beyond dissonance. No grown up children
could find their own way without some conflict of separation from their parents.

Conflict is not a contest. Much of our time and energy is drained away by turning conflicts into battles.

We get furious, we attack, we defend ourselves. We fight contests over and over again in our agitated minds. We miss the opportunity to find out what each particular dissonance can tell us. We do not see how our graced coping with conflict will enable us to deepen the divine gift of peace or consonance.

Dissonance summons us to widen our horizon. If we rise together above our discord, we shall grow to a higher vision. Conflict is an opportunity to mature in compatibility, compassion and flexibility. Fidelity implies the acceptance of the pressures of passing dissonances. Think of diamonds. Without the pressures, they would never have attained their beauty.

Fidelity to the gift of dissonance demands that I accept the challenge of each conflict and its unique message for my life. I must not deny its sting but think about it positively. I must see the dissonance for what it is—a passing event in service of my growth.

Dissonances are the challenges God sends to keep us awake. They prevent us from succumbing to the complacency of an untested fidelity. Without dissonances we may die long before we are physically dead.

Jesus' life made visible for us how to deal with conflicts in a way that does not hurt people unnecessarily. He carved out a path of peace in the midst of conflict.

The risen Lord enables us to find deeper consonance with the souls of those who oppose us, even if we cannot agree with their actions or their words. To seek for some accord is an alternative to hurting those who have hurt us.

The Mother of Jesus, the Queen of Consonance, wants us to be faithful to her son's longing to foster through us peace between God and humanity, humanity and cosmos, individuals and communities. She asks us to let go of old unworkable dispositions, to give form to alternatives for living more harmoniously. This will increase not only our inner peace and joy but effect a breakthrough in our everyday meetings with others.

Fidelity to the grace of consonance is not merely a faithfulness of the mind. It is above all a fidelity of the heart. We must allow our heart to experience the living depth and breadth of graced consonance or peace. After all, fidelity to consonance is more than just an idea.

In the cosmic Christ we are called to be alive at the very heart of the universe in harmony with all that is. We offend the grace of our transformation through baptism if we restrict it merely to a conversion of our mind. Then our faithfulness to Christian consonance is reduced to a concept rather than a living being.

Once we can feel what it means to be in consonance or not, we have something to work with. We can test experientially the degree of our fidelity. We can become aware of its increase and decrease, its ebb and flow. We sense that remaining excessively angry, upset or aggressive is incompatible with being faithful to the call to live in peace.

Slowly we become more able to spot and reform directives that lead us into irrational anger or worry. When conflicts emerge we realize that grace offers us a chance to calm down, an opportunity to renew and refine our fidelity, a chance to befriend the challenge Providence allows in our life.

We can flow in peace with the unique divine dignity of all people, even when we cannot agree with their deeds or ideas. In this deeper peace, family, friends and community can withstand the onslaught of conflict and dissension. The grace of a deeper peace enables us to survive the unavoidable dissonances within our own life, as well as the tensions within our relationships with others.

Conflict Beacon Bright

Conflict, beacon bright
on my journey in the night,
wayside sign
to my destiny in time.

Conflict, opportunity
to deepen my fidelity
to unfolding harmony
with a wider symphony.

Conflicts are a strain,
they wane and drain
the sweet complacency
of still untried fidelity.

Conflict calls my closing mind
to rise beyond the blind
boundaries of dissonance,
to join the dance
of opposing word and deed
until we meet
some common ground
no longer bound
to the paralyzing plight
of prejudice and pride.

Let our pride not steal
our peace, let us deal
with people in respect
for each one's dignity
granted by the Mystery.

12

Fidelity, Concentration, Contraction

Conflicts, if solved in fidelity, advance our spiritual life. If left to fester, they may fragment us completely. How often we are tempted to cut ourselves off from people who displease us, to withdraw in sulking woundedness from anyone who offends us.

Fidelity tries to find some bond with those who misunderstand us or whom we ourselves do not understand. The problem is that before we know it we are already moving inwardly for or against a person or situation.

To find out in what direction we are going, we must become more attentive to what is happening in our body. When we are angry with somebody, it is not only our mind that is upset. Our whole body stiffens up. It gets ready to strike at the other or to withhold ourselves rigidly. If we pay attention to our body, we will feel an inner contraction warning us that we are already beginning to move against or away from a person or situation.

Any mood, feeling, image, or disposition for or against a person or event is accompanied by some concentration of the energy that gives form to life and action. This energy directs our attentiveness in a specific way. Usually we are not aware of it unless we pay explicit attention to the train of our thoughts and feelings and their bodily expressions. The same energy that affects our attentiveness contracts in some way our mind and body in response to the moods and feelings that emerge in us. We can become aware of these, too. For example, if our presence to others is marked by warm appreciation, joy and love, we feel good. We may become aware of a gentle feeling of relaxed attentiveness, a pleasant flow of our energy toward them.

This kind of centering of our energy is mild and flexible. It makes us flow with the persons we meet, the things we have to do, without becoming anxious, rigid or obsessive. What we feel is a relaxed centeredness, guided by open and flexible fidelity. We stand ready to respond to new disclosures of the Holy Spirit demanding a new relaxed centering of our energy.

This kind of centering, guided by loving fidelity, is inspired by an appreciation of what is appreciable in the light of the Spirit. Contrary to it would be depreciative contraction. This kind of negative centering lacks ease, flexibility and appreciation. Instead of a smooth channeling of our energy, it feels like a rigid, confining compression of depreciative feelings.

Anxiety, anger, irritation, frustration, condemnation, hostility, defensiveness are congealed in a heavy lump that weighs on our heart. This lump may grow into a lasting disposition of depreciative contraction. Its density does not let through any lighthearted expansiveness, embracing forgiveness, joyous reconciliation. An accumulation of depreciative thoughts, images and feelings makes love and prayer difficult. It symbolizes infidelity to the light of the Holy Spirit whose divine generosity enables us to give harmonious form to our life in fidelity.

To be faithful to a particular situation implies that we center our overall divine gift of forming energy in a special direction. We attune it to the specific things we have to do or to the people we are called to serve. Faithful centering is not closed or rigid. It does not block the deeper flow of divine inspiration nor does it stop the river of ongoing transformation.

If we stay in the flow of God's transforming energy, we learn to appreciate any challenge that comes our way as a divine invitation. This flexible concentration represents a tranquil centering of our divine formation energy. It facilitates our coping with any venture that challenges us in the light of our fidelity to God's will in our life.

Appreciative centering is thus a full yet passing concentration of human energy. It does not diminish our readiness for change at any moment the situation demands it. We must not be paralyzed by fixation on a particular direction. Our energy must dance with the dance of the Spirit.

Appreciative centering of formation energy is beneficial. It does not deter us from fidelity to growth in consonance. Neither does it affect negatively our vital hormonal, organic and neuromuscular balance as does preoccupation with the negative side of life.

Undoubtedly, depreciative contractions are competitive, hostile, resentful or anxious concentrations of our vital energy. They are rooted in depreciative dispositions. As long as these dominate, we cannot get rid of bad feelings. We seem to be stuck in them. They cut off the flow of fidelity to the will of the Father as manifesting itself in appreciable aspects of daily reality.

Depreciation is usually faultfinding and ungrateful. For instance, we hear that a colleague has said bad things about our work. We are rightly upset. A depreciative contraction of energy sets in. We can feel it in our body. The relaxed flow of our formation energy is paralyzed too. It feels as if we are cemented in disappointment, distrust, suspicion and disapproval. There is little room left in us for seeing anything good in what we totally depreciate. We are unable to find in the other person something we can still appreciate, no matter how small or hidden it may be.

To be captured in a depreciative disposition toward others means that we will find it increasingly difficult to redirect our energy flow. Feeling secretly guilty and excessively angry, our entrapment in a depreciative disposition becomes intensified. Our body contracts even more. We are further apart than ever from the person we dislike. If we meet him or her, the other can sense us contracting in a depreciative stance. In response, he or she may contract too. Unavoidably, we withdraw from one another. Conflict becomes a contest of who can stay rigid longer in his or her contraction!

If you find that you are in a state of depreciative contraction, ask for the grace to appraise it as a warning that you are drifting away from divine appreciation, from consonance to dissonance. The grace to acknowledge an inner lump of stubborn contraction is precious. To embrace something appreciable in the person who upsets us will dissolve the lump that weighs so heavily on our heart. The Spirit will enable us to spot and affirm what is appreciable in others, no matter how veiled its appearance may be.

Much work in formation involves getting people to experience their hidden encasement in depreciative stances. They are usually not aware of them. It has become so much second nature for them that a feeling of bodily contraction seems normal. The purpose of our help should be to enable them to sense when they are contracting their forming energy in a depreciative way. Then a disposition of appreciation may begin to form itself within them.

We should always pray for the grace of whole-heartedly affirming any harmonious centering of formation energy that we experience in life. Fidelity is impossible without practicing the art of appreciative centering.

Life is a golden chain of particular events. Each one, no matter how sad or trivial it may seem, hides a spark of light. Each happening conceals an invitation to divine transformation to be responded to in trusting fidelity. To disclose and follow this faint glimmer in each particular instance demands a faithful centering of our Spirit-illumined power of appreciation of things divine in human and cosmic appearances.

Each invitation to fidelity is unique and limited. Its disclosure implies a focused centering of our energy. To grow in fidelity is to master the art of shifting the direction of energy and attentiveness to the ever-changing manifestations of God's will in our lives.

Behind the Trivia

Don't withdraw in woundedness
feeling blamed instead of blessed.
Transform the lump
of dense depreciation
weighing on your darkened heart,
make it depart. . . .
Dream the dream
of a mighty laser beam
piercing nights of infidelity
with new lucidity.
Beam disclosing beauty
of daily duty
as sharing in a mystery
that heals humanity.
Be not cemented
in resentment.
End cynical comment,
escape encapsulation
in bored depreciation.
Rise in the light
that shyly hides
in everything and happening
behind the trivia
to which we blindly cling.

13

Conflict: Source of Deepened Fidelity

While conflicts threaten our fidelity to one another, they can also be occasions for deepening it. Conflict invites us to examine the quality of our relationships. What are their strengths and weaknesses, their depth or shallowness? What is it in me that endangers my togetherness with others? What in me may lead them to infidelity?

We should not spare ourselves in this examination. How do we really feel about those near to us? Daily we meet them in a variety of moods and situations. Do we imagine that we already know the best way to approach them? Do we realize where they are coming from at this moment of their life?

The conviction that we know already what is the matter may be the greatest threat to wise appraisal of our conflicts with others. It stunts the flowering of fidelity as flexible and accommodating. Prejudice paralyzes our powers of appraisal. We miss out on discoveries that await us during attempts to understand each other a little better each time we disagree. Our ego may be too proud and rigid, our fear of failure too intense. We do not dare to stand back, relaxed and detached, to look upon ourselves and our companions in a sympathetic yet critical manner.

Only such appraisal allows us to get away from the narrow focus of a conflict. We have to rise beyond the issue that occasions our withdrawal from one another. Only then can we consider the thoughts, images and feelings that threaten the fidelity between us.

Our goal is to advance beyond the narrow focus of the conflict to a widened awareness of how the other sees the world. Such awareness sets us on the road to a solution to our separation. Treading that path, we will find deeper ranges of the other that we can share in spite of our differences. In mutual understanding, we can work toward a restoration of our relationship.

This does not mean that we say we are wrong if we remain convinced that we are not. Restoration of lost fidelity is not a blind concession or capitulation. It means, first of all, that we work toward reconciliation before we have resolved our disagreements. When we are reconciled as persons, we can progress toward a solution of the issues on which we disagree. In many cases, it may consist of a relaxed agreement to disagree agreeably. We are more able to do so when we feel nestled in the shared shelter of a deeper togetherness.

Against the background of regained fidelity, the debated issue will no longer loom so large. It begins to look less significant. Together we try to create a livable compromise. We thank God for the gift of conflict, for it provided an occasion for us to get to know one another on a new level.

Our spiritual life should be the deepest ground of our togetherness. God brought us together to be good for each other. He calls us to share in the goodness he himself extends to all. Is it so hard, then, for us to bear lightly with our differences?

We are not created in isolation. God connected all of us as members of one family in Christ's mystical body. Called to this togetherness, we should strive repeatedly to resolve our conflicts in fidelity to one another and God.

How dependent we are on such faithfulness! Take a woman who dreams about owning a home of her own. If she tries to realize her dream by herself, she may not go far. She has to involve architects, contractors, plumbers, carpenters and bricklayers. Their faithfulness allows her to build the home of her dreams. To be able to inspire them, she must see herself as a member of a group of faithful allies giving form to her future home. They in turn do not work for profit only. Were this the case, they may be tempted to cut corners, use inferior material and allow for shoddy craftsmanship that is cheaper to hire. That is why, after agreeing on a reasonable profit, they should give themselves in creative fidelity not to moneymaking alone but to the task at hand as inspired by the woman who hired them. Then a solid house can be built.

Fidelity is the guarantee of loving appreciation. It is a source of lasting peace, of fun and cooperation between enthusiastic people—a true symbol of the kingdom to come. Fidelity turns conflicts from contests into sources of new understanding and togetherness in Christian love.

Vibrant Sources of Fidelity

Conflict hardens my heart.
Destroy the barrier
that makes it the ward
of a snapping terrier
that threatens those who approach it.
Destroy the barbed wire
around embers of fire
of loving fidelity
that once was ours
in bygone days
in which we celebrated
at the bay of life
togetherness that radiated
into our souls.
Fear of failure
imprisons us;
withdrawing anxiously
we turn conflicts to contests
instead of opportunities
to test ways of mending
our differences.
Lord, grant a bending
to this crude offending.
Make us grow in understanding
of vulnerability behind stubbornness,
of rage behind resistance,
of pain behind withdrawal.
Restore us to appreciation

of what is good in people.
Rekindle companionship, collaboration,
as pointers
to good things to come,
when conflicts will be lived
as vibrant sources
of deeper fidelity.

14

Conflict and Shared Fidelity

If you watch the Bill Cosby show you will enjoy scenes that humorously portray conflicts between family members side by side with shared fidelity. All give vent to their feelings. Talking about them gently and reasonably, sometimes humorously, one or the other manages to soften his or her position. The wheels of faithful togetherness that were halted begin rolling again. The family members succeed in solving their conflicts because they try to live in fidelity to their commitments. They seek a workable solution each time discord emerges. They do not pretend they do not have disagreements. They do try to talk in a conciliatory fashion, seeking the common ground in compromise.

Sometimes we may experience an especially tough test of our fidelity to cooperate with others. This happens when we run into a wall of obstinate resistance. Obstinate people do not show us their best side. Yet we can strive to approach them kindly in fidelity to their hidden, better side. If we are sincere, we might even bring out some of what is best in them.

We should look for the hidden sources of others' obstinacy. We may discover that their anger and upset represent a release of stress. Often people who are obstinate may really be crying out for the love and attention they feel is missing in their lives. This awareness helps us to see their situation differently. A new view of what is happening may make it possible for us to approach them more wisely.

For example, Mary, the teenage daughter of a couple I know, refuses to come home at the reasonable hour they have set for her. She seems unwilling to understand that her parents want her to be faithful to her own good name, health, school work and future. It might be helpful to think a little more about what makes it so hard to deal with Mary.

One wonders if her parents sufficiently expressed their love for her in ways she could understand. What about other members of her family, her brothers and sisters, along with her teachers and fellow students? Have they shown a genuine interest in her stories, questions, problems, joys, disappointments and worries? Do they give her quality time to tell her story? Is she perhaps trying to force their attention by her obnoxious ways? Does she feel deep down that any kind of attention, however angry, indignant or anxious it may be, is better than none at all? Did her parents for too long treat her as a little child? Is she now getting back at them by staying out late every night? Is this an expression of her frustration? Or is she reacting this way to other pressures outside of the family? What about her peer group?

Thinking this way can prepare her parents for sitting down with her at an appropriate moment in which they and she can talk things out lovingly yet forthrightly. Such talk may restore shared fidelity to directives meant to foster her unique life call.

What if we discover that we are persons who often evoke conflicts? If this is the case, we should ask ourselves if we are the victims of a disposition that tells us that we have always to defend our battle stations if we are to survive meetings with other people. Are we ready to attack them or to defend ourselves? If we act that way in thought, feeling and fantasy, our conflict stance will betray itself in our posture, tone of voice and facial expression, even if we do not say openly how we feel. Others will sense our irritation no matter how well covered up it may be. They react in like manner. We react in turn to their reaction, and so it goes. We become more anxious, defensive and irritable. A new moment of tension and conflict may arise, threatening our shared fidelity to a common task.

We should examine the thoughts and feelings that almost automatically emerge when someone expresses a view different from our own. What is going on in our heads? Do we find ourselves instantly attacking their view or defending our own?

This merry-go-round in our minds of anxious attack and defense makes relaxed cooperation impossible. It arouses conflict and verbal violence. When we are always defending our own opinions or attacking someone else's, present or absent, we begin to feel isolated and lonely, threatened and insecure. We feel like early pioneers must have felt in their covered wagons arranged in a defensive circle when attacked by swarms of hostile tribes. Instantly we distrust a different way of doing things. Our imagination whispers to us that "they" must be enemies of true faithfulness to the cause.

For example, new members of the local church to which we belong may propose some changes in the way people should support the congregation. It seems to us as though they are betraying fidelity not only to the way in which "we" have always done things but also to what our local church stands for. We do not take the time to think the matter through, to see if our first reaction was right or how we can find a reasonable compromise.

To solve our conflicts, we must believe in the fidelity of God to us. Divine fidelity is never absent. It courses through all events. At any moment, we can connect with God's loving power. It offers itself constantly to humanity in conflict as a source of peace and security. To contact it, we have to renew the faith, hope and love granted to us in baptism. Our life is always linked with the fidelity of the Holy Spirit who fills the universe. Our worst illusion would be that we exist in isolation from God's loving fidelity. It is this that makes us most insecure.

A basic insecurity lurks behind many conflicts. Those who attack us may do so out of insecurity. The more we attack back, the more threatened, shaky and unstable they may feel. Our opponents may be driven to do harm to us or to our family, good name or work. If anything, we should help our opponents feel more stable, less threatened. Therefore, we should abstain from any trumpeting of our own success. Neither should we overwhelm others with our cogent arguments, impressive stories or counterattacks.

The chances of resolving our conflicts will increase in the measure that we diminish people's feelings of insecurity. We must constantly ask ourselves the question, "Does what I am saying or doing make other people more secure or less secure?"

The more we are blessed with success and recognition, the more we may be perceived as a threat to insecure people who receive little acknowledgment. This is the stuff of which many conflicts are made. Some persons, threatened by our success or talents, may be on the lookout for any occasion to diminish us. What moves them is not so much bad will as an anxious attempt to save the little security left to them in a society that levels people. Modestly hiding our successes may lessen such tempting occasions. It is much better to be a "humble mouse in the Father's house" than a roaring lion in a touchy environment of well-meaning but insecure people.

Divine fidelity wants to fill all of us with a deep feeling of security. Its presence softens the wounds of conflict and insecurity. A culture may hail this mystery in song and dance, popular wisdom, art and poetry. Some of its expressions may be distorted or strange. Yet from under the disfiguration the graced awareness of a saving presence may shine forth.

Because it is difficult to express how we feel about things, we may often be misunderstood by those who hear us. They hear something entirely different from what we tried to say. The word "obedience," for instance, may mean for some a reasonable and relaxed following of legitimate authority within the limits of one's possibilities. One feels obligated to obey only when asked something that falls within one's power. For others obedience may mean a blind enslavement to an irrational parent or boss. No wonder they feel threatened when obedience is preached to them without clarification.

Choosing our words cautiously, patiently waiting for others' understanding or misunderstanding is more charitable than rattling on. Yet our compassion should never deteriorate into a commiseration that compromises the truth.

Everyday experiences of conflict can teach us the greater ease and economy of flowing with, rather than resisting or fighting back, as long as moral directives do not demand it. The Holy Spirit can teach us how to go toward others in shared fidelity rather than against or away from them in constant conflict. This "movement toward" may enhance our fidelity to God's unique gifts in our opponents and to the enterprises we are called to serve together. What initially may seem the most ineffective thing to do may prove to be the most relaxed, effective response of all. So let us see everything in life, even its many conflicts, as a rhythmic dance directed by divine fidelity to human unfolding. It is up to us to respond in freedom to the invitation of grace to turn conflicts into opportunities for growth in shared fidelity.

Endless West of the Unknown

Lord, make me believe
in the better side of those
who bring me grief.
You are the keeper
of their deepest "why"
escaping my myopic eye.
Are they crying out
for love lacking on the route
of their lonely journey?
Can they not get along
because they were abused by some
who sinned against their dignity,
betrayed their blind fidelity
or drained them in a sea
of empty do's and don'ts?

Do they speak their won'ts
to release a secret stress
that makes them less
able to bear with life?
Are they crippled by the strife
to survive obstacles
that as barnacles
slow down their lonely ship
in clouds of mist and foam?
Why are they so alone?
Dwellers without home,
travelers in desert lands
roamed by hostile bands:

endless west of the Unknown.

The song of your fidelity
sings in this irritated life,
magic electricity
kindling the strife
to pave a smoother way
for those who went astray.

Let me gently flow and bend
with those who went
on a journey
strange to my taste.
What seems to be a waste
may lead still to a place
of peace and grace.

15

Firmness and Fidelity

Grace is given for the transformation of our life. Our faithfulness to transformation meets with obstacles. Some are minute. They may go unnoticed. We may feel tempted to delay writing a letter to a friend who needs encouragement. A small discomfort makes us neglect a cordial word to a colleague. Worries about small matters cause us not to listen with full attention to the story of a child.

It is the accumulation of such matters that may delay our growth in fidelity. They are stumbling blocks impeding our journey to the land of likeness with the Eternal. Their power lies in their repetition. A congestion of tiny betrayals of grace hinders our takeoff like an accumulation of ice crystals on the wings of a plane.

What of the larger hurdles? They may seem overwhelming. If not rightly appraised, they may stall the flow of life as drawn upward by the Spirit. Any hurdle, large or small, should be turned into an opportunity for growth in faithfulness. We cannot do so by ourselves alone. We need gentleness and firmness which are gifts of the Spirit.

The gift of firmness does not take obstacles away. Neither does it absolve us from the burden of trying to do the best we can. An effortless life without friction is

an illusion. It would be a flight from the challenges facing us during our pilgrimage.

The gift of firmness readies us to welcome impedi-
ments. We see them no longer as sources of distress.
Rather we celebrate them as invitations. The Lord invites us to turn whatever is difficult into an occasion
for growth, love and surrender. Refusing the grace of
firm fidelity, we run away from these hurdles. We do
not welcome them as opportunities.

We can learn from men and women who walked
this path before us. Thérèse of Lisieux became a great
saint by fidelity in little things. Another example is the
Venerable Francis Libermann, son of a Rabbi. Once
converted to the Catholic faith and ordained a priest,
he expanded the religious community of the Spiritans,
protecting and enhancing their spiritual, academic
and missionary traditions. He did so under the severe
opposition of one-sided interest groups inside and
outside his community. They would try to destroy one
or another of these traditions in favor of the one in
which they happened to be involved. He wrote about
fidelity in the midst of these obstacles:

> All the works that have been undertaken
> and carried through in the Church have had
> . . . difficulties. . . . Yet those difficulties
> did not scare off the apostolic men who initi-
> ated the projects, nor did they prevent them
> from going ahead with constancy as well as
> success. It has always been the way of provi-
> dence to manifest itself in the midst of obsta-
> cles and the happiest results have normally
> lain beyond the greatest handicaps (N.D. 8,
> 92, Adrian van Kaam, "Firmness and Gen-
> tleness in the Spirituality of Father Francis
> Libermann," Spiritan Papers, No. 21, De-
> cember, 1987, pp. 59-84).

Libermann suffered many obstacles in his life. As a seminarian he was affected by epilepsy. As long as the attacks continued, he could not be ordained. The illness often left his speech impaired. Some callous seminarians referred to the condition as a kind of insanity. Therefore, he was not able to continue his preparation for ordination. He was allowed to stay on in the seminary as a messenger and menial aid. His illness brought on moments of depression, but he overcame this obstacle by abandonment in faith. He also removed resolutely anything that might tempt him to suicide. He banished sharp objects from his room. If he had to pass the bridge over the Seine, he would run fast to prevent the temptation to drown himself in the river.

As a friend reported: "He never spoke about it except to help someone else who was suffering, too. Once he told me: 'I suffer an awful lot; it feels like something is torturing me and tearing my insides apart. It's frightfully painful.' And while he was saying this, the lines on his face showed clearly that he was enduring unbearable distress" (N.D. 1, 299).

Libermann's hypersensitivity inclined him to react with impatience and even with violence. It was fidelity to grace alone that enabled him not to give in to his emotions. As another person observed: "When you saw the terrific emotion that shot right through him and the continual calmness, poise and earnestness that characterized him, you easily realized how much violence it took to give himself entirely to God" (N.D. 1, 303).

Another said something similar: "It always seemed to me and everyone else who knew him that he was naturally sincere, openhearted and highly considerate, but that he was also temperamentally sensitive and quick-tempered. Time and again you could see him fighting to control his natural tendencies. Sometimes his explosive character made him react too quickly to a situation and he showed it momentarily, but a second later shame and self-mastery took command" (N.D. 1, 307).

When we read this we may feel, "But what about us?" Libermann was a person exceptionally graced, a man chosen to be a great spiritual master for church and humanity. God may grant such messengers special graces. He may enrich and beautify not only their interior but also their external life. For he may want to make them more effective and appealing in their apostolic endeavors with critical people. But what of us who are not called that way?

Our fidelity to trying the best we can without fully succeeding pleases God. He pours into our soul interior graces in spite of external failures. How surprised we shall be when we discover in the hereafter how he adorned our soul while letting us stumble on in tedious fidelity with few visible accomplishments.

Libermann would have appreciated our predicament. As he wrote to one of his spiritual directees:

> You do have a difficult character, a troublesome temperament. Don't get it into your head that you absolutely have to get rid of it. Convince yourself rather that God intends you to live with that enemy. . . . What can you do? Your nature is very bad, but you must live in peace and humble submission to God as far as that's concerned. . . . Don't be unhappy with your lot. Your natural imperfection is compensated for by great interior graces that you aren't aware of, graces that get results in spite of the bad features of your character. . . . That is why you are quite wrong in thinking that the feelings of

remorse you refer to are reproaches that our
Lord is addressing to you. No, my dear fellow, Jesus doesn't speak to your soul so
harshly. He loves you too much for that. . . .
Don't talk to me about breaking your character. . . . You don't break iron; you soften it
in the fire. Don't be in such a rush to shake
off your fault. Don't long for it too vehe-
mently . . . that would do you more harm
than good. . . . Don't take things so much to
heart. Forget yourself and quit all this self-
analysis. All these troubles will then disap-
pear gradually (N.D. 7, 35ff).

How consoling these words are to us who experience little improvement in spite of our fidelity. Some
are born with a tranquil, attractive temperament. Others develop a balanced character, pleasant and easeful
because of the wonderful surroundings of their child-
hood. They were perhaps cherished in a well-to-do,
devout family, admired by their teachers and class-
mates for their athletic, social and learning abilities,
their innate charm. But many of us were not blessed
with such good genes or with a loving, peace-filled environment early in life. Our genes or our environment
may have condemned us to ceaseless struggle for a
lifetime. No matter where we go or what we do, we
may evoke trouble. We may be known to other people
as difficult. We may not have received exceptional graces for visible transformation. Often these are re-
served by Providence for men and women who have
been destined for a special mission to church and humanity.

How can we persevere in fidelity when the fruits of
our efforts are hidden from our eyes and those of others? Why not forget about the whole thing? Why not
choose an easy life? Let our anger explode without at-

tempts at mitigation? Our slight improvements are
barely noticeable to anyone, including ourselves.

We must believe that they are noticeable to God.
Jesus loves us for our faithfulness in trying. Would
you not be happy if your child tries to please you in her
awkward way while messing things up because of her
lack of proficiency? It is not the achievement, not even
the child's effort, but the love behind it that touches
your heart.

Fidelity is not measured by achievement. Its deepest motivation is not the improvement of our personality and its social acceptability. These are worthwhile
goals. If possible, we should realize them. But the
deepest motivation for fidelity is our desire to please
Jesus. If we get it into our head that the only purpose
of fidelity is to get rid of our difficult character and of
the unpleasant aspects of our temperament, we are on
the wrong track. We are not really abandoned to
God's will for us. For he might intend that we put up
for a lifetime with our unpleasant personality, while
trying in faithful yet relaxed fashion to better it as
much as possible.

As long as we try to be as faithful as we can be, our
soul is transformed by the Holy Spirit in the image of
Jesus. Avoid feelings of false guilt and self-
condemnation. They interfere with trusting surrender
to him alone. Bear humbly with the imperfections you
cannot overcome. Maybe you will never be able to heal
the defects of your personality. Jesus does not care as
long as we live in fidelity to his love. For him it is only
our trying in love that counts. The rest, to paraphrase
T.S. Eliot's poem *The Four Quartets*, is not our busi-
ness.

Beyond the Rim of Sadness

Firmness, fidelity
blend into the strength
of a mighty stream
drowning each weed
that impedes ascendance
to a land of likeness
beyond the rim of sadness
of a faith within
that is wilting,
deadly and dim.

Burdens become blessed
invitations invested
with light
to guide the flight
to the skies
of Eternal Love.
Less and less
a source of distress,
they become a request
to turn defeat into occasion
of transformation
of the hungry heart.

16

Fidelity and the Inevitable

There are pitfalls and problems in life we cannot solve or avoid. We must flow with them in ways that do not diminish but rather enhance our fidelity to the mystery of God's presence in our unpredictable journey.

The *inevitable* accompanies our life more often than we care to admit. Threatening our sense of mastery, it appears in many forms. We may be struck by accidents, pain, illness, death. We may be faced with physical handicaps, mental and emotional blocks, divorce, loss of loved ones, breakup of friendships, loss of reputation, unemployment, bankruptcy.

What about unchangeable stress situations, addictions, irresistible temptations, bad dispositions and stubborn compulsions, the blues, discouragement and despair? Granted, by change of attitude some of these may be overcome. In that case, claiming inevitability would be a lame excuse for our desertion from spiritual warfare.

Calling "inevitable" what we can change is a disguise for our refusal to grow in fidelity by battling the obstacles on our path. Yet at times the truly inevitable will stare us in the face. We may not like to admit its presence because it betrays our secret dream that we are in command always and everywhere. If we cannot do it alone, then we imagine we can do it with the aids of experts—scientists, counselors, therapists, doctors, lawyers, even self-help books. Somehow we fantasize that we can always manage. But the inevitable is precisely inevitable insofar as it cannot be managed. What we can change is our attitude toward inevitable events, not the events themselves. Dying is dying, an earthquake an earthquake, losing a leg is losing a leg, no matter how we feel about it.

Crucial for our happiness is how we respond to the unavoidable. It determines our gain or loss in the spiritual life. Fidelity to all events as invitations of God will help us to let him use them for our transformation.

In the midst of inevitables, we are called to grow in fidelity to him who did not prevent such turns in our pilgrimage. To be sure not all inevitables are negative: Some are pleasing gifts we gratefully accept. All, positive or negative, are signposts on the road of realization of the beautiful life form God intended for us from all eternity.

How do we handle obstacles we cannot control? Do we try to deny them in order to save our feeling of having it all together, of mastery? Do we acknowledge them, find a meaningful place even for failures in our faith-filled journey with the Spirit?

Nobody can prevent certain people, events or things from affecting our life negatively. We have no power over them. We cannot bypass the inevitable. We must decipher its meaning in the conviction that all happens for the best. God's faithful directives for our transformation are hidden also in happenings we do not like, yet cannot change.

To grow in fidelity we must first of all admit that we are not all-powerful. Neither we ourselves, nor medicine, psychology, therapy, counseling, welfare, social work, nor any science or technique can change all adversities.

Perhaps our mind is contaminated by a too optimistic expectation of medical, psychological, social or economic miracles. Maybe we overestimate the possibilities of self-actualization, self-help, success tapes, will power, positive thinking, human potential. Such expectations, if overwrought, make us believe that we can get rid of everything unpleasant. Fantasies of omnipotence prepare us poorly for dealing with what is unchangeable in real life.

An example of the inevitable is chronic pain that cannot be relieved by medicine. Persistent pain is a question mark. It is like a riddle or puzzle we cannot immediately solve or make sense of outside of faith. Each responds to the enigma of suffering in his or her own way. Some may feel disappointed in their faith in God's fidelity to them. If God really cares, why should he allow this useless pain? They angrily demand an explanation of what cannot be exhaustively explained, for the ways of Providence remain shrouded in mystery. Others may believe that God through this pain is testing their own faithfulness to him in the midst of misery. Others again believe that God uses suffering to open us up to new vistas of deeper meaning and detachment.

Medical science dodges the enigma of pain. Doctors envisage pain as something to be traced to a definite cause that can be removed. Pain is an annoyance alerting us to a dysfunction somewhere in the body that can be relieved through changing its conditions.

This optimistic view sounds plausible enough when we deal with acute pain. It is not helpful when we are exposed to suffering that never leaves us. The meaning of pain becomes a real question when it cannot be removed or relieved. When faced with chronic pain, doctors and nurses feel empty-handed. They do not know what to do or say. They have been prepared to cure or to relieve. They are not there to help us seek the meaning of suffering and how to live in fidelity to this deeper sense once it is disclosed and accepted.

We may tell sufferers to be strong, positive, up-beat. These can be helpful attitudes. But they do little good without the work of acknowledgment and acceptance of sickness, death or suffering in fidelity to our divine destiny.

The ultimate inevitable is death. Usually our first reaction is denial. It is not nice to talk about death in civilized company. Yet fidelity to the reality of being a creature implies that we must acknowledge the finitude of life. This facet of fidelity is severely tested when someone is told that it is over, that one can expect to die from the illness that struck him or her.

Some are panic-stricken when facing death. Others resist but grow to the insight that the reality of death can give a deeper meaning to life. For them it does not hollow out their fidelity to the final demands of a life that is ebbing away. Instead of making life meaningless, it makes every moment richer in meaning. In the face of dying, they deepen their fidelity to life's final opportunities for purification, detachment and spiritual intimacy with the Mystery. Life appears more precious than ever. This happens when fidelity to life is grounded in a deeper fidelity to the God who grants life and takes it away in his own good time, transforming the person in the process.

Another word for this deeper fidelity to the source of life and death is faithfulness. Faithfulness means literally full of faith. We are full of faith that God through Jesus has redeemed us and that we are filled with God's own love which is the Holy Spirit given to us. The fuller our faith, the more faithful we can become to any facet of life and death God allows to happen to us. Ours becomes a graced fidelity to a horizon far wider than the body and environment we are invited to leave behind.

This deeper fidelity helps us to deal with a subtle feeling of desertion that may pervade the sense of dying. Through all kinds of experiences, such as increase in divorce, abuse or abandonment of children, war and persecution, loss of friendship, the frosty impersonality of neighborhoods, clinics, hospitals, mills and offices, we suffer today from desertion anxiety. We fear nothing more than to be left alone in this cold, competitive civilization. Desperately we cling to the few sources of affection, compassion, concern and understanding left to us in a matter-of-fact, businesslike world. Desertion strikes at the roots of our affective security. All that diminishes the affective quality of our life, already so impoverished, is experienced as a threat to life itself.

Often the fear of death is really a fear of deserting the ones we love and who love us. Those we leave behind do not know how to deal with the feeling of having been deserted. In some sense they may feel betrayed by the loved one who passed away. God is faithful to both the dying and the living they leave behind. Trust in God's fidelity can relieve the secret taste of betrayal.

Does fidelity deepen in terminal patients? For many death is experienced at first as an intruder. Initially, they deny the inevitability of the end. A battle then ensues between fidelity to the forward movement of life and bending it in another direction. We are invited to change the task of living into that of dying with dignity, in abandonment to the Mystery.

Terminal patients are engaged in a process of piecemeal, bit-by-bit leave-taking. They must take leave of everything and everybody dear to them. Their mood may change from resistance to resignation, from discouragement to hope, from anxiety to abandonment, from doubt to faith, from sadness to surrender. They must take leave of everything, even their own healthy body, their clear and vigorous mind. Both begin to be clouded by slow decay.

Dying is a parting from superfluous memories, ambitious plans and idle anticipations. Self-deceptions and prejudices are unmasked when brought into the light of the eternal. During a lifetime of busy action, curiosity, greed and ambition, the original openness of the child in us has been veiled and buried. The epiphanies of the precious here and now of life and world were seldom celebrated.

The time of dying is a time of detachment and purification. It restores the openness of the child to surrendered adults. Their vision of dying is no longer impaired by numerous cares for position and possession. Some may have been clinging furiously to dreams of glory before this forced and final recollection of the sickbed. One's public life, with its benumbing complexity of protective screens, slowly unravels. Ambitions, pretenses and defenses are peeled off one by one. Make-believe postures are softened. The heart is mellowed. If one is faithful to this mystery of transition, the core of life becomes more transparent. One grows in openness to the rich simplicity of the here and now.

A husband may enjoy the silent nearness of his wife more intensely than ever—a unique experience in the sad autumn of a shared life that is running out. What is close by, near at hand, intimate, reliable and of this day becomes far more important in its hidden splendor than faraway valuable things of tomorrow.

Fidelity to this ending and ebbing life gains a new

and strange intensity. Life detached from its acciden-
tals becomes more pure and transparent. A wondrous
disengaged fidelity to life becomes suffused with an
emerging fidelity to the demand of endmost abandonment. The inevitability of death is clearly faced now.
Death begins to be welcomed as a release from the
weight of temporality.

If this gift of purified fidelity becomes ours, dying
is no longer a fatal event. It is a sublime process of transition, of release, of letting go of life, a final rite of passage, a choosing for the end in peace-filled surrender.

This passage is not without pain. The way of fidelity that preceded this final venture enters into its un-
winding. Therefore, we should begin to grow toward
this enrichment of fidelity long before it must carry us
to the end of our odyssey. This preparation is even
more compelling because many of us may not be
granted the luxury of the recollection a sickroom offers
its terminal guests. We may die suddenly. May death
find us ready in deepened fidelity to meet the Eternal.

The Sublime Event

Who can predict a journey
directed by a mystery
transcending space and time?
We mime
its mastery, its power,
pretend that we can flower
by cleverness alone.
We lose our home
and confidence the moment
the terminal event
enters the flimsy tent
of earthly plan and project.
Proudly we reject
sad loss of mastery,
resent to bend the knee
for what surpasses infinitely
the passionate attempt
to bind the end
of cosmos and humanity
to the history
of human ingenuity.
But wait,
no trying can evade
the ultimate end of dying.
No amount of crying,
no counts of medicine
nor the hope to which we cling
can take away the sting

of the approaching end.
We may pretend
we are not touched
but soon rebuffed
by slow decay,
we fight to stay,
till idle dreams
are washed away
by gentle streams
inviting us
to another shore.
Mellowed to the core
we surrender,
the heart grows tender,
childlike again.
Power seems a main
hindrance to gain
in purity of vision,
in loving decision
to flow with the event
that brings to an end
a life of illusion,
that finds its conclusion
in a transparency
revealing the clarity
of its beginning,
losing everything yet winning
the epiphany of each moment
preparing the sublime event
of transformation in abandonment.